Long Befc

Albert Clayton

Transcribed and edited by Micah Duckworth
from Albert Clayton's original manuscript

Cover Art: detail from a painting by Albert Clayton
Cover portrait by L M Dufty (Greta Clayton)
with thanks to Barry Clayton

Map extracts in section headings from
The Daily Mail bird's-eye map of the British front
reproduced under Creative Commons Public Domain Mark 1.0
Original copies of these maps were found with the author's documents.

First Edition

Independently published by MJ Duckworth
www.longbeforedaybreak.com
info@longbeforedaybreak.com

ISBN 978-1-9163544-0-1
eISBN 978-1-9163544-1-8

Editor's note

With thanks to
Gabriel Duckworth, Mary Duckworth and Richard Grange
for assistance and advice in speeding the book to publication.

Special thanks and love to Anne, Alice and Esme
for putting up with all the typing.

Foreword

I was visiting our Mum's house, my brother Gabriel and I sorting through the room that was Dad's old study – full of antique books, documents and art materials. I slid open the cupboard under the sink and noticed for the first time the rectangular cardboard box at the back corner of the shelf.

Retrieving the box, we leafed through its contents – mostly hand drawn illustrations for magazines. We recognised the style as that of Dad's cousin Albert Clayton, and his wife Greta; both had been professional artists, and when Greta died in 1989 Dad was left their possessions. This box was typical of the countless sketchbooks, paintings and papers that had been put away for another day.

Lying at the very bottom were two old fashioned ring binders with a large stack of handwritten papers. We began to read. One of Greta's short stories maybe? There was a war theme; mention of sergeant-majors and trenches. Written in the first person, we began to wonder – could it be Albert's writing – war stories? More reading, chapter after chapter, and it became clear this was a detailed memoir of Albert's service in France beginning in 1916. We marveled at the discovery. We had no idea of its existence.

One binder had a patch of mould where it had lain for years against the bottom of the box. It was eating through to the pages inside; ink fading, paper crumbling. We cleaned the worst of the pages and set them aside. The next day my brother and I returned home.

New Year 2020, and we were together again. Albert's story had been on our minds. We decided to sit down and type the whole thing out. As some pages were still fragile and parts hard to read, we tried to recover the words. The writing was neat and readable, corrected and edited in places – evidently presented to be read by others – probably for sending to a publisher.

As we read aloud and typed, our minds were transported to France over a century ago. After several days we reached the end; pleased to reveal a complete work in four 'books' with 20 chapters; none of the words lost to decay - but ourselves a little lost for words.

Born in 1895, Albert was brought up around the cotton mills of Accrington in Lancashire, before going to Leeds School of Art. By 1916, as a student aged 21, he was recruited into army service as a common infantryman in the Royal Fusiliers.

From information in his text it is apparent he was writing sometime after 1931, possibly between the wars. By then he would be a qualified creative artist, endeavouring to write a 'piece' in the way he might produce a painting: composed, well crafted, with faithful reproduction. In general his commentary is restrained and objective in presenting scenes and events as he saw them, allowing us to take our own impressions and meaning. In accented dialogue he sketches the character of his army comrades; not turning our eyes from the bloody horrors of their front line ordeal, nor letting us dwell on them. He is keen to show there was humour and humanity, even beauty in his war experience.

This is not a war diary, but a story narrated from memory. Albert leads us with him through war-torn French villages and battlefield trenches; scenes full of graphic and sensory detail. These range from the routine daily preoccupations of army life to the blistering intensity of trench battle – culminating in an incredible tale of survival amidst extreme adversity.

The manuscript we found is unnamed, so the title 'Long Before Daybreak' is chosen from Albert's own words as he reflects on the prospect of going 'over the top' for the last time.

As far as we know, his story was never published and we can only guess the reason. Perhaps it was eclipsed by the advent of WWII; perhaps the cathartic process of writing had achieved a mental release and laid some ghosts to rest; perhaps he intended to write more, but the manuscript was put away in a box and life moved on.

We might wonder that this remarkable book only came to light after the major WWI centenaries are recently passed; though to echo one of Albert's themes, he might say this was Fate or Chance at work in some unknown way. It was only after typing up the manuscript we became aware of the film '1917' and its imminent release.

It is important that our individual and collective remembrance of this war can extend beyond anniversaries, and now his work has come to light we can be hopeful that Albert's vivid and engaging account keeps the images and bitter lessons of war alive in our minds for new generations to understand and appreciate for themselves.

Albert's life after the war is discussed in the postscript. A demobilisation certificate shows that he left army service in 1919, and exactly a century later in 2019 his story has been discovered and now, for the first time, it can be read ...

Micah Duckworth
February 2020

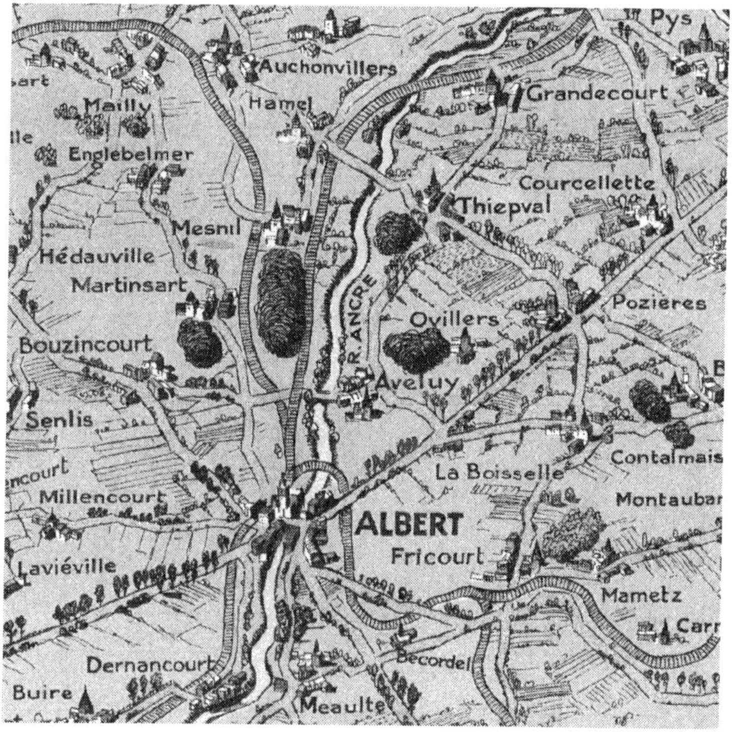
Pys
Auchonvillers
Grandecourt
Mailly
Hamel
Englebelmer
Courcellette
Thiepval
Mesnil
Hédauville
Martinsart
R. ANCRE
Pozieres
Ovillers
Bouzincourt
Aveluy
Senlis
La Boisselle
Millencourt
ALBERT
Fricourt
Laviéville
Mametz
Dernancourt
Becordel
Buire
Meaulte

Book 1

1

About twenty-four kilometres from the busy port of Boulogne and up a muddy estuary, lies a huddle of malodorous cottages straggling around the frowzy skirts of a couple of redolent breweries, a distillery, and a church of insignificant architecture. This smelly little place, Étaples by name, used to be in years gone by much favoured by the older generation of artists. The generation that etched delicately in the Whistler manner; or sat on camp-stools throughout the long summer days, vaguely trying to capture in watercolour wash the racing cloud shadows as they sped up the estuary; or daubed more boldly in ambitious "oils" at large canvases depicting statuesque fishwives performing some homely task in and about their red-tiled, tumble-down hovels.

The results of which artistic activity would appear annually upon the august walls of the Royal Academy itself, entitled "Sunlight, Shadow and Sand," "Falling Tide, Étaples," "Fisherman's Sunday Morning," or perhaps more poetically, "The Madonna of the Bay."

Apart from these staple industries of brewing, fishing, and posing for the artists, the town held little else of note; unless one includes the ancient steam tram of open toast-rack design, which ran hourly - and still does - through the scattered, sweet smelling pine woods as far as fashionable Le Touquet-Paris-

Plage over the estuary. On the Boulogne side of Étaples there stretched for miles an apparently illimitable desert of rolling sand-dunes, sparsely tufted with stiff wiry grass interspersed here and there by occasional clumps of wind-stunted pines.

By the time of which I write, namely: the historic month of July, 1916, this vast sandy waste had been transformed overnight, as it were, into a scene of feverish activity comparable only with the din and bustle of an oil strike, or of a gold-rush town in the throes of a boom period. For here, flanking the estuary, lay that amazing concentration of military zeal, the Base Camp of Étaples - known to those thousands who passed through it on their way to the Front, as "Etaps".

A mushroom city forced up by the needs of war, it comprised a ramshackle conglomeration of canvas marquees, tents, corrugated Nissen huts, plain wooden huts, stores, wash-houses, dining-halls, canteens, latrines, shooting ranges, bomb-throwing pits and model trench systems, all planted with such confusing regularity amongst the shifting sand-hills that the poor dumb fool of a "rookie" just out from England and a stranger to it all, needed only to stray a few paces from one familiar spot to become totally lost in the labyrinth.

There was in addition a heartily detested parade-ground which passed under the name of "The Bull Ring". A sinister sounding name and one far too appropriate for a place that always seemed to be stiff with roaring, bull-necked sergeant-majors forever strutting up and down the sandy arena bawling at the sweating mobs of khaki-clad cannon fodder, all marching, doubling, wheeling, left turning, right turning, forming fours, forming two deep, listening fearfully the while for the rasping word of command that would set them all marching in some new direction again. If ever there were hell upon earth, that Bull Ring was it.

If ever a moment were welcome, it was the moment those boring exercises finally ended for the day. The moment when at last the fiery-tongued sergeant-major gave his long-deferred order to "form column of route" and march back along the hot, sandy road home again. Home, that is, to the temporary refuge of one of that multitude of tents where sixteen men slept in a circle, feet overlapping in the centre, sixteen rifles hanging on the tent-pole, sixteen packs tightly stuffed with all their present belongings and forming a hard pillow that might, after all that sweaty marching, have been stuffed with swan's-down for all the impression created upon sixteen drowsy heads.

Then there was always the daily business of getting something to eat… never very easy. At times, even, developing into a rough-house scrum in which the less pushing participants got left with an unfilled mess-tin and a long, dreary wait to the next meal-time scramble.

Not, mind you, that the Government were starving the troops. Far from it. But amongst those hungry hordes that filled the dining-halls, you had to grab your own and keep a firm hand on it, or someone else would grab it first... In which case you were just "unlucky".

Naturally, the impatient thousands had to be fed in relays, so while one relay, tight-packed into the wooden dining-hut, polished off everything eatable put upon the trestle tables, at least two more relays would be queueing-up outside, waiting to rush the doors the moment they were unlocked.

In military language the act of eating is always referred to as "Messing". A particularly loathsome word to use for the subject, and one only too descriptive of the manner in which the dubious messes of stew were slopped into one's mess-tin; or of the tea, tasting strongly of tin and condensed milk, which so often had to be drunk out of the same greasy receptacle that recently held the stew.

Then at Étaples, of course, there was always the sand. Everywhere and in everything, the sand. You walked in it, slept in it, found it at the bottom of your tea, gritted it between your teeth with the morning rasher, shook it out of your shirt, enclosed it in your letters home, and emptied it out of the barrel of your rifle every few hours.

A popular drill-sergeant's "crack" in reproof of some lagging recruit ran, "Hey, you there! Are you waiting fer the tide to come in?"

• • •

The summer of 1916 was a scorcher. From dawn till dusk the sun blazed down out of a cloudless, steel-blue sky, while the sweltering camp of Étaples shimmered in a haze of tropical heat and dust, raising many regrets for the cool and lovely city of Edinburgh we had recently left behind.

There were about three or four hundred of us who had been suddenly warned a few days before that we were due for France at any moment, had visited the barber for the usual prison crop given to soldiers on draft, and when the momentous departure order came, had been rushed practically non-stop by train and boat to Étaples.

I, Private Clayton, A. Number P.S.10149, of the 29th Royal Fusiliers, a so-called Public Schools Battalion, found myself numbered with that perspiring draft. Though actually more

"Public" than "Public School", the battalion did, however, contain a large percentage of students of one sort and another. Students from the newer universities, from technical colleges, business colleges, even theological colleges, plus a very strong quota of clerks from banks and city offices. A varied (and for the most part "respectable") mass of human material which six months exposure to the hardships and indignities of military training had forced into a mould of coarser pattern, whereby one was as likely to receive the blasphemous answer from a onetime theological student as from any other.

As for the art school life I had left behind, with its indifference to worldly affairs, its supreme contempt for commerce, its sudden enthusiasms, its successes, its disappointments, its strivings to gain that all-important scholarship that would enable one to carry on - all this had vanished, leaving nothing but a heavy pack, a cumbersome gun, and the expectation of an early and painful death.

To the amateur soldier, one of the most disconcerting aspects of life in the rank and file, as well as one of the most aggravating, was the suddenness with which things happened. Orders simply fell out of the blue. One might just take a casual stroll into the nearest village to buy a packet of cigarettes and return as casually to find the whole company packed up and gone, disappearing down the road in a cloud of dust.

Indeed, it was in just this abrupt fashion that we finally left Étaples after a stay of about five days, heralded only by a ginger-headed corporal who stuck his head in through the tent flap early one morning and crudely broke the news.

"Parade in fifteen minutes, full marching order," he yelled, "we're moving off!"

"Where to?" demanded one optimist innocently, thinking they would tell him.

"Berlin," came the answer, "where the 'ell d'you think you're going?"

So within half an hour they had marched us down to the railway siding, our kit and equipment hanging on our backs; pack, gas-mask, rifle, 'tin' hat and all the rest of the oddments that bow down the heads and fray the tempers of the indomitable P.B.I. (Poor Bloody Infantry); to be packed into what somebody described with unintentional truth as "lousy cattle-trucks".

And that, had I but known it, was the last glimpse of Étaples that I was to be accorded for many a long day. In fact, fifteen years rolled by before I was destined to view it again, and all I could then find of that vast military metropolis, was about ten feet of rusty barbed-wire and a battered biscuit-tin half buried in the drifting sand.

The cattle-trucks, marked on the outside, "8 CHEVAUX 40 HOMMES," were dark and dirty vans, without windows, the only entrance for light and air being by way of the open door. The wooden floor of my particular van suffered from a charred depression in the centre, where some destructive individual, careless of railway property, had once lit a fire to make a can of tea. Evidently the water boils before the fire burns through the bottom of the van.

And so, with many a weary halt and many a false alarm the train jogged slowly along, taking us nearer and yet nearer to nobody knew quite what, though everyone knew in his bones it was bound to be something unpleasant. Exactly what form this unpleasantness would take or how long before it would be thrust upon us, was a question that could only be answered by people of greater experience in such matters. For all we in our ignorance could tell, they might run these trains right up to the firing line itself (under cover of darkness, of course) and we might be expected to climb out of those doors under a whistling hail of bullets. Yes, even stranger things than that had happened... impossible as it seemed.

Certainly, a most ominous rumble in that rapidly approaching distance seemed to be getting louder and louder with every mile we travelled; like an impending thunderstorm, or the rumblings of exceptionally heavy traffic.

However, the train came to a final halt at last with one of those tremendous jerks that are so typical of the vivacious touch of French engine-drivers, and the call passed along the train, "ALL OUT!"

So throwing packs and equipment before us, we scrambled out into the glaring sunshine.

No bullets whizzed by... no shells burst around us... no Germans were in sight. In fact nothing was in sight at all but a few quiet fields extending peacefully enough towards a very straight line of very upright trees lining a long, straight road which vanished away in the distance in ever-diminishing perspective. The only disturbing element, and that still happily remote, being the faraway rumble and roll, which went steadily on.

The sight of this peaceful landscape combined with the discovery that we were not going to be rushed straight up to the mouths of the belching guns, evidently put new heart into the draft, for as we formed up in "column of route" and headed for the road they broke into song. And later on, as we eventually drew near a village, my spirits too began to revive and my interest quicken in the unfamiliar scene, while the foreign sounds and smells that floated down the breeze stimulated my senses by their strangeness to a more normal pitch of cheerful anticipation.

The execution was postponed for a space.

2

There is something very French even in the smell of a Picardy village. Not that it is in any way unpleasant or strong. But where the odour of an English village might consist of say, a groundwork of cottage-garden flowers, a whiff of beer from the "Ploughman's Rest", plus a dash of weekend petrol fumes, French village air carries a pungent tang of wood smoke mixed with appetizing whiffs of roasting coffee, onion soup, and pigs; all set against a savoury background of warm ripe manure.

The background is not surprising when you consider that the average village consists almost entirely of farms, each farm being built round a courtyard the centre of which is usually occupied by a deep, square manure-pit. The French farm has, in fact, been described as "a collection of buildings surrounding a rectangular stink". Into which, by the way, the farmer's family throw their discarded chicken-bones, out through the open door as they sit at their evening meal.

Another peculiarity of the Picardy village is the apparent dilapidation of many of the barns and outbuildings. They are built in a rustic timbered style reminiscent of our own Elizabethan work. That is to say, an elaborate framework of beams and cross-beams forms the skeleton of the building and supports the roof, while the spaces between the timbers are filled in with what looks like dried mud. We always swore it was cow-dung.

In the general wear and tear of life this primitive plaster acquires innumerable dents and chips, even gets large holes knocked in it in places. Small wonder then, that this the first village I had seen at close quarters, gave me the impression that the Germans must have been there recently, it looked so knocked about. There, plain enough for all to see, were the identical pits in the plaster made by the bullets of ruthless "Huns" as they lined up the resisting peasantry and shot them in cold blood, just as we had read in the papers. Or so I imagined.

I was not, however, to be afforded a closer view of those pock-marked walls and holey barns just yet, since the cocky young lieutenant who had met our draft at the siding and now stalked at its head, strode on through the village without a halt. So the march continued, until by and by the road began to grow rougher, to rise slightly and change into a rutted cart- track leading deeply into a forest of small trees.

This forest turned out to be our destination, and passing under the green arch of its leaves, a smell of camp cooking soon assailed our nostrils; while as we penetrated further into the forest glades curious habitations revealed themselves between the trunks. Low huts constructed of earth-filled sandbags, with walls about three feet high supporting a peaked roof of tarpaulin painted in those jazz patterns that are supposed to deceive enemy airmen. Lounging idly in the huts, which were destined to be our homes for a little while, were a few hundred men, the sole remaining remnants of the 8th and 9th Battalions, Royal Fusiliers.

On the First of July, 1916, the battle of the Somme had opened in thunder and in pain, killing ninety thousand British alone in the first fortnight. And these before us were some of the lucky survivors... We had come to reinforce them.

Cockneys practically to a man, and as hard-boiled a lot as any I had ever set eyes upon, they were at home - when they were at home - in the Old Kent Road, Commercial Road, Hackney, Poplar, Stepney, or "The 'Ditch". Full of caustic comment, always ready with a flashing retort, they were forever grousing yet forever cheerful in a contentious kind of way, their favourite lament harping with perpetual disgust upon one sore point, namely, that French beer was muck " 'Orse piddle, that's wot it is, mate! 'Orse piddle!... You can drahnd yerself in barrels of the blinkin' stuff an' never git a smell in yer breff."

Ducking our heads to enter one of the low huts on our first arrival, we were greeted by catcalls and a sanguinary flow of outspoken comment from the rudely awakened inhabitants.

"Blimey!" guffawed the heroes of Ypres and the Somme, "'Ere come these bleed'ng schoolboys!" And then, in a mock Oxford accent: "How did you leave the mater, old boy? In the pink?" It was a gag of which they never grew tired for many a long day, until the "schoolboys" themselves became automatically "old sweats" by the ultimate arrival of a still newer draft.

I have never been able to determine the exact location of that forest camp, but the nearest village of any size and importance, Mailly-Maillet, lay somewhere just north of the war-scarred town of Albert in the department of the Somme. The camp itself was situated, as near as I could Judge, about four kilometres behind the actual firing line, well out of range of anything but the biggest shells; and probably out of range of those too, for none arrived to trouble us while I was there.

For a little time, except for minor irritations, the days passed uneventfully enough. By some ill-chance I had got hold of a rusty rifle when they were handed out to us at Étaples, and if there is one serious crime in the Army, it is undoubtedly the crime of harbouring a rusty rifle.

With every rifle goes a "pull-through". A weighted cord to which is attached a little piece of oily flannel measuring four inches by two, and in addition a piece of metal gauze of similar size for use in place of the flannel when so required. The inside of the barrel is kept clean and shiny by pulling it through with this oily bit of "four by two"; or if very dirty, with the metal gauze.

Every few days a rifle inspection would be held to see if this pulling through was being done properly and the mechanism being kept in smooth working order.

The troops would be paraded in two ranks, rifle held ready for inspection with the breech-bolt pulled back, whereupon an officer would pass along the ranks, squinting in turn down the muzzle of each rifle while the victim of this inquisition held his thumb nail at the other end, thus causing a reflected light to shine up through the barrel... And woe betide the owner of any thumb nail that threw light on a rusty barrel. He was "for it" as the saying went.

Unfortunately, neither oily flannel nor metal gauze would shift the ingrained rust from my barrel, pull it through how I would; and this worried me considerably until one of the old hands at the game relieved my anxiety by indicating a possible solution of the difficulty.

"That 'bondhook' (slang for 'rifle') o' yourn," he said, "must a' come off uv a dead bloke to git as rusty as that. If I was you, mate," he counselled sagely, "I should 'lose' it quick an' 'find' another afore they crime yer for it."

So I accordingly "lost" it.

"Passing the baby" so long as you passed it to strangers was customary practice in that society, and the merest self preservation. "Don't pinch from your own platoon" being the generally accepted rule - anybody else was fair game.

I think it must have been about this time too that I first began to scratch... One of the minor irritations of the War had got me, and I felt almost proud of it... Lice! Or as they called them, "Chats!"

If, just as you happened to be conversing with a person, he suddenly appeared to go crazy, dived his hand swiftly into the neck of his shirt or the top of his trousers and scratched himself with the frenzied rapidity of a dog scattering fleas, you didn't take much notice. You knew he was only "chatty"... All real soldiers were "chatty". It was indeed an honour to be "chatty", setting one apart from those pale-faced, half-baked "base wallahs" whose duty to their country was done sitting on office stools way back in the safe areas where the smack of bullet and the whine of shell never penetrated.

A favourite spare-time occupation for men resting in dugout, barn, or bivouac after the labours of the day, was to take off their shirts or roll down their trousers in a vain attempt to reduce the ever-present colony of "chats" by running a lighted candle along the seams of the material. Crackle, crackle, crackle, popped the roasting vermin, but the task was a hopeless one, since every blanket you slept in, every sandbag pillow you laid your head upon, every bit of wood or fabric you came in contact with, was "chatty", and you would acquire a brand new colony every night.

Many were the jokes upon the subject of "chats". Some hard-shelled specimens were dubbed "mahogany-backed 'uns"; while others, larger and tougher still, were reputed to have been out since Mons, and to have gained numerous decorations for the many battles through which they had accompanied successive owners. It was claimed that the only way of discouraging the attentions of these irritating pests was to turn your shirt every half hour or so, whereupon the little beggars would die at last of a broken heart through continued marching from outside to inside again.

One day while crossing a ploughed field in the company of a party sent out on some digging operations, I saw my first shell-burst... A whirr, a bang, and a billow of brown smoke down the far end of the field made all we new comers duck our heads in alarm... and all the "old sweats" duck too; but more from force of habit than alarm... It was only a stray one. Thus gradually were the privations and dangers we knew lay in store for us revealed to us one by one, until one day, I supposed, the growing burden of discomfort would reach its peak and we should know the worst.

The weather remained fine and hot as befitted the month of July; and in the cool, stilly night, sleeping under the twinkling stars amidst that forest of young trees one might easily have imagined the circumstances that brought us there to be nothing but a figment of someone's diseased imagination, were it not that under cover of darkness the distant rumble appeared to take on a much more sinister reality, working up at times to such a pitch of intensity that the very ground beneath my head seemed to tremble and shake. Whereupon, some old soldier would sit up in the night, gaze with unseeing eyes towards the south and mutter, “Blimey! The boys are coppin’ it ‘ot dahn there tonight,” then light a fag end and lie down again.

But the time was bound to come, of course, when we too should have to travel in the direction of that awe-inspiring racket. Which unhappy time arrived all too quickly, for parading one morning in “fighting order,” we moved off at full battalion strength leaving our packs with the transport waggon - an ominous sign that we were bound for places where packs would be an en-cumbrance.

• • •

The road we took led eventually through the village of Mailly-Maillet. A fairly large place disclosing several important looking country mansions surrounded by orchards and set back behind high brick walls pierced by elaborately wrought iron gates, in the spacious manner adopted by the Frenchman of substance when he retires after a busy life to his villa “a la campagne”.

Here and there the brick walls had been demolished by some erupting force; one or two biggish holes in the road had to be skirted by our party, now moving in single file; and the church belfry towering up above the houses had at some time stopped a nasty punch in the steeple - as if some giant pugilist had tried to “knock its block off”.

Further along, the whole front of an estaminet appeared to have fallen forward on its face, scattering loose bricks and plaster all over the road, and a cloud of grey dust over everything else. The further we went, the more demolished the property became, while occasional whining noises overhead ended abruptly in muffled thuds away over the other side of the village.

Then, just as we were passing the broken walls of a house, a terrific, blasting sort of crash rent the air, making me duck my head instinctively into my collar, then gaze round at my companions to see how many were left - and how many had been turned into bleeding lumps of meat.

But it wasn't a shell after all - at least, not the arrival of one; merely a battery of our own guns firing from a camouflaged position amongst the ruins.

Leaving the ruined village behind, our road soon emerged into open country and would, if we had continued along it, have carried us straight into the arms of the enemy. So at this point we scrambled down into a narrow communication trench which started at the side of the road, and which I was to find led twisting and turning for perhaps a couple of miles right up to the front line.

About ten feet deep and barely wide enough for two people to squeeze past each other, its friendly walls engendered, nevertheless, a comfortable feeling of safety that the wide open road had latterly failed to inspire. Along the bottom of the trench, lengths of "duckboard" had been roughly laid to prevent the place from becoming the slippery drain it would otherwise have been during wet weather.

Several dangling 'phone wires looped and staked into the crumbling, earthy side had in places come unstaked and fallen across the trench bottom; thus causing each man as he inevitably caught his foot in the loop, to utter foul imprecations and warn those following behind with a blasphemous "Mind the wire, behind there! Mind the wire!" While the following man, loaded up to the eyes with his equipment, his rifle, his gas-mask, his sandbag of stores or heavy Lewis gun parts, would echo as he in turn caught his foot, "Blast the wire!" and work off his spleen in picturesque adjective.

Long grass interspersed with scarlet poppies overhung the top of the trench which led onwards, sometimes crossing other trenches, sometimes forking to right or left, sometimes opening out into a basin-like depression where a shell-burst had widened it, onwards until it reached the limit of our own particular world, the front line; the boundary as it were of the British Empire itself, beyond which no man dare go unarmed, and beyond which there lurked that malignant, alien Power perpetually trying to beat us back.

The way was long, my burden of equipment heavy, and the feet of one "Ginger" Lewis who clumped behind me, too pressing on my heels.

"I 'ope they don't shove us in support," he panted on the back of my neck.

"Why not?" I asked, "I should have thought the support line was better than the front line."

"No, not 'ere it ain't," he dissented. "When you're in front you does yer whack of sentry-go; then if the blasted Boches ain't blown any parapets dahn for you to build up agen, maybe you gits a charnce of a bit o' kip… but when you're in support," spitting disgustedly, "they 'as you workin' all the bleed'ng day fetchin' an' carryin' sacks full o' God knows what all up and dahn this bleed'ng communication trench… then all the bleed'ng night they 'as you aht in No Man's Land wiv a bundle of posts and a mallet, a-fixin' bleed'ng wire."

As a matter of course, the support line was the first trench of a defensive nature that we reached on our journey up to the front. A deep cutting about a hundred yards behind the front line, it was honeycombed on the forward side with holes leading down ten or fifteen decrepit steps into musty, earthy-smelling caves infested by rats, where the troops when off duty led a troglodyte existence, sleeping, smoking, "chatting", playing pontoon with a ragged pack of cards, or attempting to boil a drop of water for tea over a few bits of damp stick. Although at Mailly-Maillet these mouldy dugouts were mere holes devoid of any fittings, I found later on that in other places they were comfortably furnished with tables, chairs, and even in rare cases with pianos, all salvaged from near-by ruined houses.

The front line when we got to it, turned out to be a deep meandering trench cut in the shape of a squared zig-zag, so that one could walk no further than about ten yards in a straight line without having to negotiate a sharp double corner into the next bay. On the side facing the enemy a "fire-step" had been cut, allowing the sentries to stand up head and shoulders above the top of the trench and look out after dark across the dreary waste of No Man's Land.

"This is not so bad after all, Nobby," ventured one of our new draft to an older hand, gazing at the neatly revetted parapet and clean swept duckboards. "Fact, if this is all, I can stick it for duration."

"Oh, you can, can yer?" came the scathing reply. "Well, I 'ate to disillusion you, mate, but lemme tell you somethink: This 'ere place we're in nah is one of the cushiest spots on the 'ole of the Western Front... and Bucking'am bleed'ng Pallis to wot we shall get... Believe me, they've just brought you blokes 'ere to break you in easy like, afore they send you dahn there on the Somme to be slaughtered... same as wot we was at Loos while you kids wus still at school."

Which pronouncement sounded only too true, and in the long- run far from reassuring.

• • • • •

We found, of course, another regiment in occupation when we arrived in the front line on that blazing afternoon in late July (The trenches there were safe enough to allow of a daylight relief). Another regiment standing impatiently by, chafing at the delay in our coming. And the very moment our officers and theirs had formally "handed over," stood one another a farewell scotch in the officers' dugout and said their "cheerios" and "good lucks", they tarried no longer, but were off hell-for-leather the way we had come.

After all, why linger? When you have stood up to shot and shell for nearly a week you don't wait to see the next one drop... it might be that one with your name on it.

So they bided just long enough to give us their parting advice:

"Patrol that gap on your left arter dark," they said; "keep yer 'eads dahn in the day-time; watch aht for a sniper they've got in the middle; and don't light no fires." With which fruit of experience, they shot off.

The daytime in that front line did not at first seem too alarming. I just had to stand about the fire-bay with a fixed bayonet, taking a peep across No Man's Land every now and then by means of a box periscope, through which nothing much could be seen, however, except a lot of long grass and tangled wire. Behind this trench the ground rose steeply to the crest of a small rocky hillock which lay between us and. the support line, giving the pleasant feeling that we had a wall at our backs - and friends behind the wall.

The unpleasant feeling started soon after we had got settled in, with a sudden, terrifying "Whiz....z....bang! Whiz....z...bang!" half a dozen times in rapid succession. The "whiz" cleft the air just over my head; the "bang" burst itself against the rocky hillock behind; while the air was filled for the space of seconds with the hum of bees - the bits and pieces of flying iron.

Just a German "Whiz-Bang" battery administering the regular daily laxative... About once every two hours the dose was repeated, and each time it occurred I waited in fear and trembling, expecting every moment that the next one would fall short of the hillock and explode in the trench. Why the German gunners failed to shorten their range and drop the whole lot in the trench I could never make out. But by some miracle they didn't.

It was old Bill Parker, the Company's oldest soldier (out since 1914), who set my mind as much at rest as ever it was likely to be upon the vagaries of shell-fire. "Don't get the wind up, mate," he said, "for you never 'ears the shell that kills yer."

Every evening at sunset and every morning at dawn, a certain ritual known as "Stand to", was invariably performed. At these times every man jack in the Company, except runners and officers' cooks (and even they couldn't always dodge it), had to take his place on the fire-step fully armed, and stare out across the mists of No Man's Land as if to repel an attack. A practice that had arisen, I supposed, out of the need for greater caution during these shadowy, between-light periods so often favoured by the powers that be for the launching of grand-scale attacks.

On my first evening there, then, I stood up on the fire- step with the rest and strained my eyes out across the dismal void in a resolute endeavour to spot any untoward movement on the part of the wiley "Hun". But when, after about an hour's vigil, "Stand down" was ordered, my turn of sentry duty had unfortunately come round and I was constrained to remain where I was for several hours more.

According to the brusque instructions of the sergeant who posted the sentries, I was directed to "Stand up there, see?... and keep yer bloody eyes skinned... an' if yer see anyfink movin', 'oller aht, see?... an' if any bloke comes along the trench, give 'im the "Alt! Who goes there?' and show 'im the point of yer bayonet... see?"

I leaned my elbows on the top of the parapet and peered into the gathering dusk, over towards a low rocky ridge about a quarter of a mile away at the foot of which the German trenches lay.

As the long summer twilight slowly faded into night, the No Man's Land in front of me took on with the dwindling light an ever-deepening mystery and horror. To my distorted vision, that dreadful, gloomy waste seemed to be filled chock full of incredibly tangled, rusty barbed wire half hidden in the long, dry grass; while the lumpish wooden posts to which the wire was fastened, seemed never to remain in the same place for two minutes together as I vainly tried to count them in the dark. At one instant they would root me to the spot by their remarkable resemblance to men, and the next, freeze my blood to ice by their fancied disappearance into the earth like prowling beasts.

Beneath the disordered scrabble of grass and wire, the ground was pitted with old, weed-grown shell-holes, tenanted by a stinking army of putrefying corpses left to rot where they fell during an unsuccessful attack of many weeks ago. For although this was now a quiet part of the line, it had not always been so.

If only these gruesome reminders of previous failures had been as dead as they smelled, I could have contemplated their remains with a peaceful mind. But they weren't...

There were noises. Curious noises. Little, almost imperceptible rustling noises flickering to and fro amongst the putrescent remains. Something alive was there as well, sending a chill of fear down my spine. A mystifying something that kept on moving the stiff, dry grass and shaking the wire, impelling me to take a firmer grip on my rifle and bring my bayonet up to the "ready", finger crooked round the trigger.

Rats... and monsters too! But only rats, thank heaven!... They were after the pickings.

Peering closely at the nearer remains I could see how busy they were. Scuttling here; scuttling there; popping in at the mouth of a gaping corpse; popping out again at a tear in his tunic... over his leg... tug at a bit of cloth... stop and listen a moment, bright eyes shining... disappear for a time in the shadow of his body... then down to his foot and into the interior again by way of the top of his boot.

Ceaselessly scurrying, ceaselessly hurrying, so ran the tenor of their abominable lives.

• • • • •

Without warning a sudden, rocket-like swish gashed the night and a ghastly, blue-white light shot up into the sky, illuminating both wire and corpses for the space of several seconds as a Verey light fired from further along the trench, soared, and burst, and fell, and spluttered to death out there.

As the blinding glare died down, an enemy machine gun roused into activity by the soaring rocket, started to traverse the top of our trench, its "rat-a-tat-tat" echoing across the empty waste, its fire creeping methodically along the line until, as the sound drew near, I was forced to duck down behind the parapet and await the passing of its sweeping stream of bullets... Then I arose and continued my vigil.

Apart from the startling whiz-bangs, there was little actual bombardment of our positions. Down south, however, along the desolate strip of No Man's Land towards Beaumont Hamel, I could see that history was being beaten out in blood and iron, for in the night the horizon flashed and flickered incessantly as if lit by distant blast furnaces, while the surging roar resembled the pummelling of a thousand mighty hammers in some titanic forge.

They were attacking again on the Somme, as they did almost every night.

A sudden clumping of heavy boots on the duckboards behind me, and I wheeled swiftly round with the challenge I had been taught, "Halt! Who goes there?" rising to my lips.

"Righto, kid. It's me, Sergeant Downes," came the gruff reply. Then in a hoarse whisper, "Wiring party just goin' out on your right. Don't shoot!"

And a few moments later I saw them... creeping out amongst the rats and the corpses of No Man's Land, trying hard not to clank their implements together as they went... creeping out with their posts and mallets and rolls of wire to add a few more yards of entanglement to the wilderness already there.

Listening hard, I could hear a muffled thud... thud... thud as they drove their wooden posts into the ground, a piece of sacking wrapped round the top of each post to deaden the sound of the mallet.

And then, as another soaring star-shell lit up the scene of operations from the enemy's side, the thudding ceased. They were standing stock-still until it subsided again; by so doing, hoping to remain invisible to the enemy sentries.

"Stand still, and they won't see you," was the reassuring dictum; but it took a lot of faith to remain bolt upright in that glaring light.

How slowly that first night the weary hours wore away!

How far away the people and the places I had left! How remote the possibility that I should ever take up the old life again! How interminable the processes of wearing down the "Hun"! How inconceivable the victory! How distant the end! But above all, how certain the inescapable destiny of us all, and how improbable that any of us would still remain alive to witness the end!...

Until at last I heard with pleasurable anticipation the feet of the relieving sentries come clumping along the duck- boards. A few moments later they clumped into my bay, one of their number took my place on the moonlit fire-step, and I was free to withdraw my anxious gaze from the phantom-haunted wire and drop back into the friendly protection of the trench.

My first spell of sentry-go was ended and it was with the greatest of heartfelt relief that I stood down. I relinquished the post with alacrity.

Anybody could have the job, for me.

3

Just as we were on the point of leaving that front line at Mailly-Maillet after a stay of about six days, I was ordered to report at once at the Company-Headquarters dugout. Wondering a little what sort of a job I was going to "click" for, I did as directed, and found the officers' cook, ugly as sin, standing outside the dugout door just in the act of slinging a string of pots and pans round his bull-neck, ready to take his jangling departure.

A sullen-looking, thick-lipped cockney, he squinted at me out of little piggy eyes and demanded abruptly, "Are you the bloke wot's bin sent to give us a 'and?"

"Well," I replied, "I was told to report here, but for what I don't know..."

"That's a'right then," he cut in, churlishly, "we'll soon show you wot for. Grab 'old o' that there mess-box," pointing to a long, black, coffin-shaped, wooden chest of no seeming light weight, "an' shove orf with it!"

I seized the rope handle dangling from one end of the box while Blackall, one of the officers' servants, seized the other, and we hoisted the heavy object on to our shoulders prior to staggering off with it down the long communication trench like a couple of undertaker's assistants.

The Company Headquarters, whose servants I was thus called upon to assist, needs here a word of exemplification. It consisted of the Captain, on whose responsibility lay the command of the Company; of his four lieutenants, more light-heartedly commanding the four platoons; of their personal servants, each amateurishly valeting his "boss"; of a cook, who did his best to serve up to the five officers as "Ritzy" a menu as food supplies and his limited knowledge would permit; and of the two "runners", or "Company Orderlies" to give them their proper designation, who acted as messengers, guides, water-carriers, and unofficial scroungers in general of anything required by the Mess.

This select little party of servants, cook and runners, usually managed to secure for themselves the best of what was going in the way of food and lodging... if there was any best.

The driest dugouts in the line, the pleasantest farmhouse billets out of it, and a share of the appetizing "left overs" after the officers' table had been served, enough to make the mouth of the rank and file soldier dribble with envy.

The knives and the forks, the plates and the dishes, the utensils which the cook used in his processes of boiling and stewing, besides the tins of provisions, loaves of bread, joints of meat and other items employed in catering for the more exacting palates of the commissioned ranks, were all carried about from place to place in the coffin-like mess-box. Consequently, it was always filled to bursting point, generally had to be held shut by an encircling rope, and weighed heavy as lead.

Bearing his end of this not inconsiderable load, Blackall strode on in front of me, his 'tin' hat tilted rakishly over one eye, his head pushed out of the vertical by the awkwardness of our burden, his sunburnt neck exuding beads of perspiration with the exertion of carrying the box.

Though something of a dandy and rather fond of "poshing himself up", Blackall remained withal, a brawny enough fellow. But I, being by nature far from brawny, found supporting my end of the box much more fatiguing than he did; not to mention the awkwardness of doing so while endeavouring to retain a hold on my rifle which persisted in slipping off my shoulder. So before long I was compelled to call a halt.

"Whatever have you got in the damned box to make it so heavy?" I asked in some exasperation, as we dropped it for a breather and leaned panting against the side of the trench.

"Pots an' pans it's supposed to be," he replied, "but if you arsk me, Bert - that's the cook - 'as got 'arf 'is bloomin' kit in there as well, the lazy perisher!"

"Oh he has, has he? Why the hell don't you tell him to hump his own damned kit, then, instead of breaking our backs with it?"

"Tell 'im?" he echoed disgustedly. "You don't know Bert. 'E's as bad tempered and stubborn as a mule, that bloke is. You can't tell 'im nothin'."

"But surely," I protested, "it's not right that we should have to carry his stuff..."

"No. Of course it ain't right. But I'll tell you why we don't say nothink... 'Cos 'e dishes aht the grub, see?... 'e dishes aht the grub. An' so long as 'e dishes it aht all rahnd, share an' share alike, we don't take no notice of 'is funny little ways... No, 'e can shove 'is blasted gran'mother in the box provided 'e 'ands rahnd the rub-a-dub dub... Besides, I'd do the same meself in 'is shoes. Anybody would."

So reflecting ruefully upon the sad philosophy that when the grub is scarce it's the hand that serves the skilly that rules the roost, we picked up the box once again.

All went well for a time. In spite of the weight of the box and of the hot sun beating down on us in the narrow trench, we maintained a steady pace until, after about a mile of smooth going, we struck the inevitable trouble; and like half the troubles we had to put up with, it was due not so much to enemy action as to muddled organization on our own side. Someone had "mucked up" the times or the routes again, and as a result another relieving company were well on their way up the wrong communication trench; the same one down which we were departing.

Although the trench was just wide enough for two persons to pass comfortably in the ordinary way, the continued brushing-by of large numbers of men loaded up with equipment waxed aggravating in the extreme to both parties. But for us, bearing the box, the feat became a torment of the damned.

Sweating, swearing, growing more and more exhausted every minute, we pressed forward, while hundreds of savagely cursing troops squeezed past the box. Meanwhile, our own exasperated Company were pressing on behind us, chafing at the delay and consigning both us and the box - when they discovered what was causing the hold-up - to the gaudiest of imaginable fates and the most lurid of destinations.

"Christ, I'm fed up to the teeth with this!" gasped Blackall at last, mopping his brow, "we'll never get by at this rate. Let's get aht of the blinkin' trench an' take the perishin' thing over the top."

"What? Get out in the open with it? You must be barmy," I declared. "What about the Boches?" I asked. "Won't they see us?"

"Well, wot if they do? It's a long way off an' they'll be lucky to 'it us fust shot... besides, we can 'op back in the trench if they start on us."

So with some trepidation on my part, we lugged the box out on top, every moment expecting to hear the whine of an enemy bullet come chasing us back into the trench. But the distance was great and we went unobserved after all, doing the rest of the journey in comparative ease and comfort. By the time we reached the road, however, I was so utterly exhausted by our strenuous efforts that I had to sit down on the box to recover.

"Put yer 'ead dahn between yer knees," advised Blackall, "you'll be all right in a minute." Which I did.

And that was the last I saw, or ever wished to see, of the trenches at Mailly-Maillet.

• • • • •

"It's a long way to Tipperary," sang our late lamented predecessors of 1914, though by 1916 that particular song had become as dead as the men who first gave it fame.

Nevertheless, it might have described the succession of marches that followed our departure from Mailly-Maillet although the distance was not great - heading always south towards that grim shemozzle now taking place on the Somme. A peregrination that presented a monotonously recurring series of cool, shady woods, flat fields, rusticated hamlets, curious pavé roads with a dirt track down the side for walkers and cyclists, all leading us finally to a small village on the high, moorland ground just behind the shattered town of Albert; pronounced "All bare" by the local inhabitants, who sold us eggs and coffee and glasses of grenadine or vin blanc.

There was a lot of straw on the floor, I remember, as I sat cleaning my rifle in the upper storey of one of the village barns. Many of those timber and plaster erections contained a sort of attic storey nestling in the rafters as it were just beneath the crazy, red-tiled roof, reached only by means of a vertical ladder up the outside, difficult to climb with a full kit, and generally minus a rung or two.

It was at the top of one of these ladders that the boiled-beef face of Company Sergeant-Major Williams appeared on the morning in question, like a big red sun rising through fog - he was partial to his drop - commanding us all in no uncertain terms to "clean up an' shine up," there was going to be a very special parade. "Very special indeed... and Gawd 'elp the poor bloke wot comes on parade with one spot of dirt on 'is equipment!... Gawd 'elp 'im, I say, for 'e'll ruddy well need it!"

After making this sinister pronouncement the Sergeant-Major removed his turkey-cock face from the opening and clattered noisily down the ladder again.

"Now what's the old buzzard mean by that?" we asked one another. "Surely they're not going to put us through one of those 'spit and polish' parades we used to do in England. Not here, surely, so near the line."

Some seemed to think they were, however, and that such a fuss could only mean one thing: that some very big bug indeed must be about to treat himself to a look at the pawns he moved about so easily from away back at Army Headquarters. Maybe the General of Division; maybe the Corp Commander; maybe the Commander- in-Chief himself. Who that individual happened to be at the time I neither knew nor cared.

Then the King was rumoured. But general opinion seemed to be against this idea. It couldn't be the King. "Garn, they'd never let 'Is Nibs get as close as this, would they nah? Besides, wot's 'e want to come aht 'ere for when 'e can stop in Bucking'am Pallis an' read all abaht it in the papers?... Would you come, Nobby?... Would you, Ginger?"

Chorus of "Not me's. Not bloody likely!"

All the same, we were in due course paraded around the village square, carefully examined back and front for any tarnished brass or grubby tunic, marched up the road a short distance - just out of reach of those long range guns, I suppose it was and then lined up on both sides of the road in proper ceremonial style.

A long, boring wait followed, to be relieved at last after an interminable time by a rustle of movement from far down the road, like the sudden stirring of leaves which precedes a storm. A crackle of sharp commands then surged along from the seat of excitement, to reach us almost at once in the form of an order barked out by those qualified to bark.

"Pre-sent hup!" ran the stentorian command. And smartly we "presented hup"... Upon which the largest collection of "Brass Hats" I had ever seen together in one spot hove in sight, moving majestically along the middle of the road like a cloud of bees in search of somewhere to swarm.

To the plain "Tommy" a "Brass Hat" was a being from another world. A gaudy wasp to be approached warily and saluted smartly with an extra loud slap of the hand on the rifle butt. An officer so high in rank that the very sight of his glittering hat bearing those twisted masses of gold braid, mesmerized one into behaving like the automaton a common soldier is expected to be. And here, strolling nonchalantly along, were at least thirty of the species all in a bunch.

With my rifle held stiffly upright in the "Present Arms" position about one inch in front of my nose, and hardly daring to move my eyes, I squinted past its wooden stock at the glittering crowd.

Amongst the moving flock I marked one figure, rather shorter than the rest, whose profile struck me by its likeness to a penny: George the Fifth.

Further behind and centre of another little constellation strode a boyish figure of somewhat puckish mien overshadowed by a service cap that looked too large for him - as mine had always felt - and who no doubt gave some of those "Brass Hats" many a bad quarter of an hour trying to keep him out of danger: Edward, Prince of Wales.

And so they passed. A flash of gold braid, a blur of khaki, a wrinkled brow, a gesticulating hand, then, taking not a blind bit of notice of we who lined the route, these chimeras from another world drifted by and were gone.

• • • • •

But we were not to remain long in the safe back areas. The morning after our glimpse of the King we were off down the hill and soon picking our way between the piles of broken brick and plaster, practically all that then remained of the town of Albert.

Formerly a busy little town specializing in the manufacture of sewing-machines, it now lay mostly in ruins, the streets mere beaten tracks between the rubbish heaps that once were houses. It takes an enormous expenditure of ammunition to reduce even a small town to dust, so in spite of the frequent explosions that continued the pulverizing process as we passed by there still remained an astonishing number of walls and house fronts still upstanding.

Passing in single file beneath the most cliff-like of these broken walls, we gazed up in awe at the famous statue of the Virgin which once graced the spire of the Basilica, but now, held only by the feet, stuck straight out at right angles to the remains of the spire, seeming as if the slightest shake would, bring her crashing down on our heads. This remarkable mass of gilded bronze had been hanging there precariously since January 1915, when a shell had hit the top of the tower and left the statue bending face downwards over the shattered square, as if counting the marching legions who passed below.

For so long had she remained in that unbelievable position that a superstition had grown up around her predicament. It was said that when the Virgin fell the war would end.

"Why the hell don't they knock the thing down then, and let's all go home," was the irreverent comment I heard as we craned our necks to gaze at her, silhouetted against the blue.

Albert in July 1916 was a hot spot in more senses than one. The sun blazed fiercely out of a sizzling sky; the air was heavy with heat as up towards the front we plodded. Unending streams of traffic choked the roads, raising clouds of chalky dust to settle in a grey film over leather equipment, khaki cloth and perspiring flesh alike, caking in a grimy line on lips too parched and dry for once to blaspheme.

Guns, ammunition carts, water-carts, ration carts, G.S. waggons carrying loads of timber and wire, jostled us into the side of the road as they lumbered past on their way to feed the voracious God of War. And all amongst it the little Red-Cross vans dodged in and out, bearing away what fleshy morsels the God had chewed but failed to pulp completely.

Nearing the one-time village of La Boisselle, our trudging file of men instinctively increased its pace to a more hasty, shambling lope as we approached a dangerous fork in the road. At this notorious fork a wooden shrine enclosing a carved and painted crucifix stood solitary by the road side, as it did on almost every Picardy road. The painted blood of Christ trickled from those sacred wounds, down a chipped and faded body, while the air around hung heavy and pungent with the faint odour of burnt explosive. An odour far too freshly made.

"Crucifix Corner" observed 'Ginger' Lewis, who had been there before. "An' it 'aint a 'ealthy district neither," he continued, as we skirted some newly-made holes in the road. "Can yer smell that smell?" he asked, sniffing the air.

"Yes. What about it?"

"Well, whenever you get a whiff o' that, my boy, take my advice an' don't 'ang abaht. Git aht of it, quick, before the next shell 'its yer...'cos there'll be one due any minute, see?"

"I bet that nose o' yourn 'as saved yer life a few times, 'aint it, Ginger?" grinned Collimore, a tall lanky youth, treading hard on my heels with his big feet.

"Yus. An' will agen... Look aht!" he added, as a whining shriek tore just over our heads. "...'Ere it comes."

A booming crash behind, and we looked back towards the Crucifix to see a billowing mushroom of red smoke rising into the sultry air from a heap of bricks.

"See?" commented Ginger, tapping his ruby, sweat-bedizened nose as we pushed on, "wha did-ah-tell-yuh."

Then, further along the dusty road, an astounding spectacle moved Collimore behind me to repeat in mock astonishment one of the most outworn of Bairnsfather jokes. "Crikey!" he said, "What made that 'ole?" And for a wonder no one answered, "Mice."

Two vast holes in the earth met our gaze, each as big as a good-sized quarry - the biggest one, quite a hundred yards across. They were the Great Mine Craters of La Boisselle and had been made by the exploding of mines under the German positions on the first of July, 1916. Around the holes for hundreds of yards were scattered the chalk boulders and stones which had shot up into the air, along with many German soldiers no doubt, on that historic day when the roar of their explosion had signalled the opening of the First Battle of the Somme. The day upon which our troops opened the game by dribbling a football across No Man's Land... But what a starting gun!

The work of tunneling under the Boche lines and exploding mines was usually carried out by sappers who were ex-coal-miners. Hard-headed "Geordies" from Durham, tough little bow-legged runts from Lancashire, or quick-tempered, loquacious Welshmen from un-pronounceable places. They would carefully and quietly excavate a long narrow passage extending well under the enemy, while those wary birds, expecting something of the sort and hearing the "tap, tap, tap," of ghostly picks under their feet, would feverishly set to work to drive a counter-sap and forestall their opponents by exploding it first.

Both sides would listen intently for the tapping of each other's picks, and pray for its continuance; for then all was well. If the tapping stopped, it might mean that the sap was finished, that the explosive was being packed in, the detonators fixed and the electric cable trailed out of the sap and away towards the plunger attachment, one thrust down of which would fire the lot and elevate the unlucky party to a seat amongst the angels.

"It drives some o' them sapper blokes balmy," remarked the informative Ginger, "listenin' fer that blinkin' tappin' to stop… Plumb crazy they goes. An' then they gets sent 'ome to Blighty with whadya think?"

"I dunno. Wot?"

"Shell-shock, the lucky perishers! Ber-linkin' shell-shock!"

4

Our battalion lived for the next few days in the open country just by the Great Mine Crater, Most of the day-time being spent in lounging in the sun near our tiny dug-outs, hollowed out of an overhanging bank of chalk, and most of the nights in carrying sacks of bombs, or digging near the front line.

The contour of the land in the Somme district is gently undulating, ridge following ridge like the swell on a calm sea; and the battle into which we were now thrown, had become a shockingly expensive process of driving the invaders back, ridge by ridge, while they clung grimly on to every dip and hollow, every village, wood and sugar-mill.

By the end of August the conflict was raging fiercely about two ridges in front of our little dug-outs at La Boisselle, and to reach the front line we had to tramp along a nasty mile-and-a-half of open road, until we reached what had been the village of Ovillers. I say "had been a village," for it was now nothing but a collection of brick-heaps, and those had been turned over and over and pounded to dust by the incessant bombardment.

Just where the communication trench dipped down from the road to worm its way between the battered foundations of houses and the relics of cellars, just there stood a shrapnel-dented water-cart marking an extremely "hot spot." Dead bodies lay about in nauseating and stinking profusion. There were so many of them inextricably mixed up with the rubble and dust of the crumbled houses, and the burning rays of a hot sun had played on them for so long that the place was nauseous with the odour of decomposition. The hot, still air, filled with the hum of flies, languished in the sickly scent of pollution and decay.

A party of us had set out with picks and spades, as we did most nights, to dig a new support trench behind the front line. Moving up the road in a straggling file, we had nearly reached Ovillers and the comparative safety of its stinking cellars, when shells began blasting the road in front of us.

"Down in the ditch" yelled the officer in charge, for there was nowhere else to take cover and that no more than a slight depression. But shallow as it was we threw ourselves down, pressing our bodies into the soil and hoping for the best.

I could hear the whir of flying iron and the thud of fragments striking the road not a yard away, but luckily, no shell burst directly amongst us.

Returning by the same route at day-break, a gang of "conchies" (conscientious objectors) at the self-same spot engaged in the thankless task of filling up those newly made shell-holes in the road. A job that had to be done no doubt, that meant staying near where the shells fell thickest but one that, along with the disagreeable one of burying the dead, was often delegated to those who objected to fighting.

"Serve 'em damn well right, the so-and-so dodgers" grunted someone, with a dirty oath.

"Garn!" came the reply from his pal, "You'd a' bin one of 'em too, if you'd only 'ad the guts."

"Well, wot abaht you," argued the first speaker? "Wot brought you 'ere, then. Some skirt 'anding aht white feathers, I'll lay a quid. Or maybe it wus Kitchener's blinking photo, pointin' 'is bloomin' 'and at yer. 'Kitchener wants you!"

Then, as the party wended its tired and dispirited way back down the vile road, somebody struck up that ungrammatical and doleful dirge:

"I want to go home, I want to go home,
Don't want to go in the trenches no more,
Don't want to fight with the Germans no more,
Oh! Carry me over the sea,
Where the Allemand can't get at me,
Oh my! I don't want to die,
I want to go ho--me."

It was mere grousing set to music, but was promptly cut short by the platoon sergeant, who turned round in his tracks and barked, "Aw, shurrup there, will yuh! Pudda sock in it, fer Christ's sake."

We had not as yet occupied any of the front line during the Somme Battle, but only paid flying visits at night, carrying supplies and digging. One day, however, the rumour went round that a big attack was coming off, and we were to be in it. Sure enough, the rumour proved true, for in the early evening we left our tiny dug-outs in full force and moved up the long communication trenches to the front line, and I noted several other units streaming in the same direction.

Leaving our packs behind - sinister omen - we stopped a moment at an ammunition dump to be handed two Mills bombs apiece.

A "Mills Bomb" is a sort of iron cricket ball filled with explosive; or perhaps, being slightly oval and deeply scored into squares on the outside, it may be likened rather to a small pineapple. The deep scoring of the outside being intended to make it fly readily into several pieces on exploding.

There is the story of the Irishman who was "mopping up" as it was called, after an attack; that is to say, he was going round the newly captured trenches to see if any armed Germans were still lurking in the dug-outs.

Coming to the mouth of one dug-out he calls down, "How many of yez down there, begorra?"

"Seben," comes back the answer in guttural English.

"Well then" says Pat, throwing a Mills bomb down the dug-out, "Share that amongst ye."

When we arrived in the front line on that September evening, - I can't be sure whether it was the 3rd or the 4th of the month - we were packed in the trench almost tight enough to touch elbows.

The officers and platoon sergeants moved along the crowded trench pointing out over the top in the dusk, the objective we were about to take. It was a German trench only three or four hundred yards away, and we were instructed to "go straight for it, hang on to it, but go no further."

We were assured that "anyway, our artillery will have blown all the occupants to hell long before you get there."

All very well, but I had heard before of this "blowing the Germans to hell;" sometimes a machine gun or two would survive the bombardment, in which case we should fall like corn to the scythe before we had gone twenty yards.

The chances, I thought, of such a thing happening, were about evens. But like everyone else, I was hoping that if anything did hit me, it would be a nice easy one through the shoulder or the soft part of the leg. Something just bad enough to get me to England in a lovely hospital, with nice nurses hovering round, and people leaving chocolates, and cigarettes, and cheering the "brave boys" as they were carried out of the train on stretchers at Victoria. Something temporarily crippling without being unpleasant. In the vernacular of the time, "A nice Blighty one."

It was commonly said by the old soldiers, some of whom had lived through from the dim past of 1914, that if your number was on a bullet, you'd get it; dodge it how you would. If the Fates had picked out a certain time and place for you to be killed, and a particular bullet to do the job, there was no avoiding your destiny. Until the hour struck, neither bomb nor shell could touch you; but at the appointed time that bullet would come round corners after you, find you out even in the deepest dug-out.

Chance is a curious thing. There is, however, such a thing as putting yourself in the way of events, inviting Chance, as it were, to have a crack at you.

I remember one fellow, an otherwise intelligent, well- read sort of fellow, but a religious maniac, who would persist in walking on top if it occurred to him to do so.

To those who adjured him to "come down you bloody fool," he would reply, "I am the Lord's anointed; I am in His care;" or some such nonsense.

Of course he got it in the end. Smack through the head with a sniper's bullet, one sunny afternoon.

As the time drew near for us to go over on that September night, there grew a tense expectancy in the air. Some were savouring a last Woodbine, maybe their last on Earth, while others were having a swig of the rum that was usually passed round on these occasions.

A Second-Lieutenant standing near me kept swinging his arm round every few seconds to look at his wrist watch, for eleven o'clock precisely was our zero hour, and on him devolved the duty of leading the way.

The short scaling ladders were against the side of the trench to enable us to get out quickly. Our bayonets were fixed and shining in the dark. The artillery were trying to be strictly normal so as not to alarm the Germans; just the usual amount of banging and crashing: no more, no less.

Then, at about three minutes to the hour, the normal shelling developed suddenly into a shattering crescendo as every British gun for miles around concentrated on that one German ditch in front of us. Shells swished overhead like express trains and as we peeped over the top, a line of boiling, heaving ground over there showed us where they were bursting. They were "blowing 'em to hell."

A few seconds after the roar started, the S.O.S. rockets soared frantically skywards all along the enemy lines, and then their artillery opened out on us.

The darkness around me suddenly became filled with shattering explosions. I was surrounded by ear-splitting crashes. A patter of small stones rattled on my 'tin' hat and a reek of sulphurous fumes burned in my nostrils.

Then, penetrating the veil of thunderous sound, came piercing wails and shouts of "Stretcher-bearers. Stretcher-bearers this way." I heard afterwards that many were hit during that ghastly three minutes, before they were able to climb out.

The Second-Lieutenant gave a last glance at his wrist watch and bawled, "Come on, boys!". Sergeant Downes, the father of his platoon, chanted "Over you go my lucky lads," as if he were running a crown and anchor board, and we climbed out.

• • • • •

I wasn't sorry either to get out on top, for the trench had become a death-trap during the last few minutes, when the German barrage fell on it.

The night was black. No moon lightened the obscurity of what was to come. The darkness of the veil of night was intensified rather than relieved by the stabbing flashes of bursting shells, and their explosions crashed so close around me that I was continually astonished to remain alive.

I saw figures dimly in the enveloping gloom, staggering and stumbling about. Whether they staggered because they were hit, or because they had tripped over the entangling wire, I didn't know. One minute I would stub my toe against some nameless debris, the next my feet would drop away into the black void of a shell-hole. Then a length of barbed-wire would claw at my legs and a splintered post graze my knees, for the place was all littered with such fragments of wood and wire, chopped up and scattered by our gunfire.

If our guns had been less efficient in breaking up the wire we might have got entangled in it and been shot to pieces before we could free ourselves. Such a calamity had happened at Loos in the previous year and the affair had become such a byword that a new stock-phrase had been added to the common speech in consequence. To any general inquiry as to "Whose seen my what's-its-name?" or, "Where's old so-and-so?" the inevitable reply would be, "'Anging on the wire at Loos."

Right from the start of my training, that grisly bogey, "Bayonet Practice," had loomed large as a frightful necessity, some day to be practiced in earnest. It had comprised mostly the stabbing of swinging sacks under the lurid anatomical directions of pseudo-blood-thirsty instructors, and the rushing of dummy trenches bravely manned by a sack and sawdust army.

Forward at the sound of the whistle we had been trained to go. Jab at the swinging sack, then on to the trench with a yell.

"In... Aht,... On guard!" bellowed the ruthless instructors. "In... Aht... On guard! In... Aht... On guard! Suffering snakes, what a mob! What a prize blinkin' mob of perishing suicides! 'Give 'im four inches in the belly,' didn't I tell yer. 'Four inches. And pull it aht quick afore 'e falls on yer.'

"Nah then, let's 'ave it agen. In... Aht... On guard! An' yell yer bloomin' 'eads orf this time, to put the wind up 'im. In...Aht... On guard! In... Aht......In......Aht......"

But I didn't want to stick my bayonet into real stomachs if I could possibly avoid it. So, like many others, I kept a round up the breech of my rifle, "One up the spout" as it was called, ready for any close contact with the enemy, and I intended letting fly with that before any German got so near that I had to stick him with the bayonet.

• • • • •

When at last we reached the German trench, the part I struck had been almost obliterated by our gun-fire, and was tenanted only by the dead and the dying. About a dozen Red Cross men wearing white armlets were trying hopelessly to succour the wounded, but as soon as we appeared flourishing our bayonets, they all put up their hands and pointed to the armlets. I too, felt immensely relieved to see those armlets, for it meant that I was absolved from taking part in any dirty business of sticking or shooting.

We jumped down into what was left of the trench, somebody led the prisoners away, and we started immediately to dig a fire-step in the side, ready to resist any attempts to recapture the trench. I peered over the top into the darkness and loosed off a round or two of ammunition in the general direction of Germany, for though there was no definite target to fire at, I felt that I couldn't go through a big battle like that without having a pot at something. And up to then there had been nothing at all to shoot at.

After a time the firing died down a little, so feeling safer from any immediate danger, we began to look around and put the place in shape the better to resist a counter-attack. While I stood on sentry-go, some of the others got rid of the dead Germans by grabbing their arms and feet, and slinging them out over the top.

In the process a fine German pistol came to light and was promptly claimed by a sergeant. I stepped down for a moment and joined the group who were craning their necks round the sergeant as he tried in the darkness to examine the find, when, "Rat-a-tat-tat-tat-tat," it suddenly went off in his hand.

Luckily, he was pointing it downwards at the time and the stream of bullets embedded themselves harmlessly in the ground. Later examination in daylight disclosed it to be a beautifully made automatic, holding twenty cartridges which could be fired singly or, on pressing a button at the side, the whole twenty streamed off like a machine gun. It was the button the sergeant had pressed in the dark.

Time and events unrolled themselves that night with the unreality of a dream. The extreme nearness of death seemed to lift every occurrence on to a plane of childish nightmare, where unnatural things happen and yet seem natural. Where Death's finger touching you, causes neither surprise nor sorrow. And the mind moves so swiftly on these exalted occasions that the speediest of events appears to unroll itself with the ponderosity of a slow-motion film.

One dramatic flash-back to that night remains etched on my memory. A soldier being handed two German prisoners to take back behind the lines, and his reappearance very soon afterwards, minus the prisoners.

"What 'eve yer done wiv 'em," somebody asked?

His reply, "Oh, I just shot the b.......s, I wasn't goin' back all that way with 'em," was accepted without comment as quite a natural part of that "Midsummer Night's Dream."

As dawn tinged the sky, our surroundings took on a more earthly aspect and the cold light of day gave form to the place we had captured.

In certain places a jelly-like quivering of the ground puzzled me at first, until I realised that it was due to the presence of dead bodies lightly buried by the caved-in sides of the trench. They had been interred by the shells that had killed them.

Scattered about the intact portions of the trench were rifles, spades and accoutrements of a strangely different pattern from our own. Coal-scuttle 'tin' hats, grey-green tunics, and little pork-pie caps piped with red braid, all possessing that alien cut and colour which we had hitherto viewed only through periscopes, and learned to associate with those queer "robot" figures at whom we shot.

Evidently our sudden onslaught had surprised them soon after the rations and post had arrived, for several pieces of dark-looking bread and a number of unopened letters lay scattered about, forgotten in their extreme haste.

We opened some of the letters, addressed to "Oscar this" and "Franz that," and found them written, of course, in a language none of us could properly read. Some of them contained photographs. One in particular I remember of a plumpish, middle-aged woman and two little girls in pigtails, all sat up stiffly conscious of the camera amidst the photographer's velvet drapings. It was signed across the bottom, "Deine dich liebende Frau."

I wondered if his "loving Frau" would ever see him again, or whether he was one of those we had slung out over the top last night.

The counter-attack which developed against us in the morning provided a big moment for Regimental Sergeant-Major Saunders. Though young for the job of running a battalion, maybe thirty-ish or so, Saunders was a frighteningly slick individual of electrifying personality. His cold, smooth efficiency fed by his insufferable conceit, seemed to jerk his tall immaculate figure into an insolent swagger. No back could be more ramrod, no poise of head more arrogant. And that steely gaze emanating from below a rakish 'tin' hat, could, even at a distance, hypnotize one into a self-conscious fit of the fidgets; set one's fingers searching for that undone button.

The attack developed not, as it happened, directly against us, but against our 9th Battalion who held a trench to the right and somewhat in advance of ours. A sudden call had come for bombs and yet more bombs to be passed up to them, while all along their sector a straight wall of flame appeared. The "Boche" were trying liquid fire.

Immediately the rapid passing of those bombs became a vital factor, and Sergt.-Major Saunders the man who saw to it.

During the night a connecting trench had been dug from our old front line to the new, but there had not been time to dig it more than three feet deep. Along this shallow ditch the bombs had to be carried in sacks, each man shambling along in a stooping position to avoid the spray of bullets the "Boche" were directing over it.

Saunders knew his part to the letter and took his cue with suitable dramatic emphasis. Squatting down on a heap of gravel at the trench junction, his tilted 'tin' hat just below the whistling bullets, he directed the passing of the bombs with his waving revolver.

Flourishing the revolver threateningly, he announced in his light tenor voice that he would "Shoot any b........r that stopped passing."

Nobody stopped. Though all were exhausted almost to the point of collapse, the urgency of the occasion kept the sacks of bombs on the move. Mechanically I accepted sack after sack passed on to me, in a dream carried them a few yards along the trench, and in a mist of exhaustion passed them to the next man and returned for more. My feet clung to the earth with weariness as if held down by the pull of a quick-sand. I was not built for such heavy labour and in consequence suffered agonies of fatigue where the professional navvy would just perspire a little and curse. And of such dull, insensible toil does war mainly consist.

The liquid fire attack was successfully repulsed, we were left in heavily shelled occupation, and new lines, I supposed, were drawn on the maps at Headquarters and published in the newspapers for my apprehensive family to read at home. I learnt later that we had captured the Windmill of Pozières, though at the time I didn't know the place for Pozières and saw not the vestige of a windmill.

Three or four days more we remained there, gradually getting dirtier and dirtier, water being too precious to use for washing. We had to fetch it in petrol tins from that isolated water-cart away back on the much-shelled road in Ovillers.

Once, the fellow who had gone to fetch it failed to turn up, so I was sent after him with two more petrol tins, down the long, winding, broken trench to Ovillers. As I climbed out on to the road, there in front of me stood the solitary water-cart. There also, slumped down in the dust, lay the missing watercarrier, both he and his petrol tins riddled with shrapnel holes.

Hastily, with ears cocked for the whine of the next shell, I filled my two tins, lingered a moment longer to fill my own water-bottle, and returned with relief to the comparative safety of the trench.

The nearest shave I had during those few days occurred in the front line, when a flying shell splinter struck the butt of my rifle with a whack, chipping a lump out of the wood about one inch below my hand.

"Coo, blim-e-e, mate! What a cushy one yer missed there," said my companion of the moment. But being an artist I preferred to keep my hand, though most of the others would willingly have sacrificed both hand and arm to get out of the show.

At last the happy day arrived when our places were taken by a fresh lot of troops and we could make our way back to Ovillers, past that fatal water-cart and down the shell-holed road, past our roaring guns still "giving 'em hell," on to the busy plain of La Boisselle, there to he met by, of all things in the world, the Regimental Band. Its ten or a dozen men - "lucky swines to miss the show" - played us along the dusty road with many of the tunes that have since become wearisome, not forgetting that hackneyed regimental tune of many obscene parodies, Colonel Cody.

When they finally lined us up for a roll-call to see how many were missing, the basilisk eye of Saunders rested upon a rag-taggle mob of dirty, bleary-eyed tramps; rested strangely without comment, upon tarnished brass and unbuttoned tunics, and on stubbly beards sprouting out of faces so grimy that the sweat had washed rivulets in the dirt.

The most pressing need was for a drink and a sleep. Especially a sleep, for during the last night or two of sentry duty, we had had to jerk one another back to consciousness every few minutes with a nudge in the ribs; every nudge starting visions in my mind of the things that happen in the history books, to sleeping sentries.

And so ended, with a long-deferred sleep, my first experience of going "over the top." First time lucky.

5

But all was not blood and thunder.

I have since listened to people describing their travels in Syria, their happy hours in sunny Malta, or how they got drunk in the brothels of old 'Stamboul', and the fact becomes clear that the war gave to some people, the time of their lives. Though on further inquiry it usually turns out that those same lives were rarely in danger.

Even France, that insatiable, yawning grave, had its tranquil retreats, its "cushy" little jobs well behind the travail and the fray. Quiet little backwaters off the mainstream of operations, where a few lucky individuals would continue for years to perform some very essential, yet pleasantly safe occupation.

Spending their spare time playing poker or pontoon with a few pals. Sipping vin blancs or strange liqueurs in quiet estaminets, picking up the while, a few French phrases from Madame's piquant daughters; or teaching them to lisp vulgar English ones.

For every ten men dodging shot and shell in the dirt of the trenches there had to be one more fortunate somewhere behind, handling the bombs and the bully-beef, the boots and the blankets, the timber and the Tickler's jam. Repairing lorries, driving Staff cars, developing air photographs, drawing maps, or maybe just blacking out the indiscreet parts of our letters to "Dear 'Sister' Ann."

Many also were the ex-clerks who had escaped from monotonous jobs, dull suburbs and perhaps nagging wives, now enjoying the open-air life and the prestige of wearing an officer's uniform. Those two or three pips on the epaulette could confer upon the meekest of men, a consciousness of the power of rank, with all its saluting, and its "Yes, sir," and its "No, sir," and its "Very good, sir," and its "Where's my blahsted servant gone with my damned valise?"

Even for us poor "foot-sloggers" who bore the brunt of the strife, there had to be periods of rest and recuperation in some quiet flower-grown part of the line, where men only got themselves killed occasionally by some freak of ill-luck.

It was to such a place that we went after the Pozières attack. Marching back through the crumbling town of Albert, under the still unfallen Virgin and through the pleasant villages of Picardy, northward towards Arras.

Stopping at one of those rustic villages after a hot and gruelling march, I had just thrown off my heavy pack and equipment, down with a thud on to the earth floor of the barn which was to be our billet for the night, was just cooling off after humping all that load, when a corporal poked his head in at the door.

Leaning through the wicket he inquired, "Which o' you blokes is Clayton?"

"That's me," I replied, cursing my luck at having "clicked" for some job of work, as I thought.

"Report to Company Headquarters, the Cap'n wants to see yuh, toute de suite." ("Toot sweet" he pronounced it).

"Me? What for?"

"They've got a job for yuh, kid, that'll just suit yuh."

"What sort of a job?"

"Ther's a new Comp'ny runner wanted," he explained, "owin' to the last bloke 'aving stopped a packet at Pozziers, an' you bin picked for it."

I didn't want the job. In my ignorance I tried to persuade the corporal to choose somebody else, but he wouldn't; said he'd been ordered to fetch me. So, very reluctantly, I went to the farmhouse where the Company Officers were billeted and saw the Captain.

"Righto, Clayton, you'll do!" he said, glancing up at me through a cloud of cigarette smoke. "Just bring your kit over and stick with headquarters in future. Crabtree will show you the ropes."

So I had, perforce, to do it.

Crabtree was a fellow I had known slightly in the Public Schools Battalion in England. Smallish, very dapper, round head with bright rather protuberant eyes, and very rosy cheeks. Though his age was probably nineteen or twenty, he looked more like a perky sixteen just joined up from school.

Two runners were always attached to the Company Commander and his headquarters, and they were fond of picking the youngest in the Company for the job. Hence, Crabtree and I.

My initial distaste for what turned out to be an interesting job, was purely psychological. So far I had scarcely come into contact with any officers, but on those occasions when I had done so, they had behaved in such a rabid, snapping dog manner that my rather bashful, Art School-trained personality had been scared off. I was intimidated by the general overbearing manner of the class and by their curt, peremptory way of addressing the common soldier; extremely conscious of the many taboos, of the standing to attention when addressing an officer, of the perpetual saluting, and all the rest of the invidious nonsense which is specifically designed to uphold military caste.

But I need not have worried. Most of the "Pukka Sahibs" of the regular army had, fortunately, been either killed off or promoted by that time, and these were the less stiff-necked "New Army" type.

The job turned out to have compensations and privileges and a freedom of movement which came as an immense relief, after the dullness of staring stupidly over the top at a lot of wire, hour after boring hour.

Instead, a sort of roving commission all over the near locality, finding out the whereabouts of every section of the battalion. From the high quarters of the omnipotent Colonel, to the humble dwelling-place of that worthy set of men, the Sanitary Squad; more familiarly known as the "Shit Wallahs."

Crabtree and I had to be ready at any time to carry the "chits" which were the chief means of communication between responsible persons in the battalion. Or sometimes we would be used as guides, to take parties of men to places where they had some task to perform.

When not employed in this way we would assist Bert, the officers' cook, in his efforts to dish up a good dinner, by doing a bit of unofficial "scrounging," and incidentally ensure that he gave us a share of it: digging up a few spuds from some Frenchman's field, cutting a nice fresh cabbage from some unwatched allotment, buying eggs or long French loaves from any farmer's wife who would sell them to us.

If we could also "knock off" a few bottles of red wine from some unguarded cellar, so much the better; for when Bert got a little oiled up he tended to be more liberal with the officers' food.

Though my lot was now cast amongst the little clique surrounding the Company officers, when the Battalion was on the move I had to march with the men as before.

Leaving the Somme behind, the road we took was not lacking in variety and interest. Travelling on foot in a long column of fours, with the Colonel at its head mounted on a horse, the Battalion wended its perspiring way through the twisting, green lanes or along the arrow-straight, tree-lined roads which connect village with village in those parts.

On approaching a village of any size, the Drum-major, strutting in front of the drum-and-fife band, would puff out his chest and start twirling his baton, while the dozen men or so who formed the band, would strike up the stale old "Colonel Cody," or "Pack up your Troubles," on their thin-sounding flutes.

Sergeants and corporals would then step out to the side of the road for a moment, calling sharply on their platoons to

"Pick up the step, there! Left... Right... Left... Right... Left... Come on, pick 'em up, there, pick 'em up! 'eft...'ight...'eft." Upon which we would hitch up our wearisome packs and try to walk a little more erectly under the shoulder-chafing load.

All this, no doubt, to maintain the prestige of the British Army in front of the peasantry, while they would cast looks of bored indifference or sometimes of black surliness, as if we had infringed the privacy of their country, and mutter a resigned "C'est la guerre."

Every hour a halt would be called and we would throw ourselves down on to the grass verge of the road for a ten minutes rest, and a puff at the inch of Woodbine carried behind the ear from the last halt. At the shrill blast of the whistle, discarded packs would again be resumed, the "Column of route" be re-formed, and at the command, "By the ri-ght... quick... march!" the rhythmic tramp of hobnailed leather would ripple along the column once more, to beat the road for another hour.

One of the officers who could speak a little French would have gone on ahead to our final stopping place, and, acting as "billeting officer," would meet us and indicate the quarters he had picked out.

For the Colonel and his staff, perhaps one of those rococo chateaux, the country house of some Parisian stock-broker, temporarily deserted by its owner. For each Company-commander and his lieutenants, usually a farmhouse. For the sweating, dusty troops, several of those timber and dried-mud barns, admitting shafts of sunlight and plenty of fresh air through their many crevices.

The barns were never empty long, being kept in continuous use by successive lots of ever-shifting troops, so most of them had been fitted with tiers of beds, made of wire-netting nailed on to a timber framework. A candle-end or two stuck in an old tobacco tin, and a worn bass-broom for sweeping the earth floor prior to evacuation of the billet, completed the furnishing.

While the officers dined in the farm-house parlour, having their meals served up to table in civilized manner with one of the officers' servants to run with the steaming dishes - the feeding arrangements for rank and file in the barn-cum-cowshed billets were not so "de luxe".

Three meals a day, breakfast, midday dinner, and tea were "dished out" practically on the floor. And if you were not there for the "dishing out" you were just "unlucky."

To each company was attached a travelling cooker, a kind of boiler on wheels after the style of the familiar tar-boiling engine. In this cooker all the water for the tea was boiled and the slushy stews concocted from heaven knows what, by the grimy-looking cook and his assistant.

It was fired underneath with coke, supported a tall, stovepipe chimney which could be folded down, and was drawn by one of those long-eared, bastard horses, an army mule. When the column was on the move the cooker brought up the rear, blowing out clouds of steam and clanking along like Stephenson's "Rocket."

In billets the cooker was drawn into the court-yard of one of the farm-houses and there, amidst an aura of farm-yard smells, the cooks did their dirty work.

Part of the cook-house equipment consisted of dixies - a kind of oblong bucket with a lid - which were used for holding hot liquids like tea and stew. These dixies would be stood upon two or three bricks with a fire underneath and when the water boiled, the cook would throw in casually a few handfuls of tea and sugar, empty into it a tin or two of condensed milk, give the brew a stir with a soup ladle, and remark with proud satisfaction to the waiting mess-orderlies, "There y'are, mate! A drop o' real sergeant-major's. Strong enough to make yer eyes knock together."

The orderlies would then grab the dixy handles and stagger off with it between them, back to the waiting platoon laying back on the wire beds in the barn. No sooner was the dixy dumped down under the archway of the court-yard than the shout went round, "Tea up!" and the lounging occupants of the barn would be galvanized into action. Hastily grabbing a mess-tin, they would queue up for their turn to dip it in the steaming dixy of tea, an N.C.O. standing by to see fair play.

If the meal happened to be breakfast, there might also be a couple of dixy-lids laid out with rashers of strong bacon fried in tomatoes. These were carried back to the barn in your mess-tin lid, or on an enameled plate, if you had been squeamish enough about eating from tin lids to buy yourself such a luxury.

All the dry provisions were brought round the billets in sand-bags. Loaves of bread with sand-bag hairs sticking to the crust, rock-like army biscuits hard enough to break the teeth of a horse, hunks of soapy cheese, tins of bully-beef - one between two or three men - tins of Tickler's jam ("pozzy") - one between six or seven. Mostly it was plum and apple, greengage, or quince. The choicest varieties such as strawberry, had already been picked out for sergeant-majors, quartermaster-sergeants and such like folk, before the rations ever got as far as the men. That was always the trouble with the rations, they passed through so many hands before reaching "other ranks" that the best had often been skimmed off, leaving precious little for the poor fighting man, nearest to the enemy but furthest from the ration dumps.

Fortunately, parcels from home were fairly frequent, and after the postman's visit, chunks of Mother's home-made cake and Aunt Flossie's flaky mince pies were passed round the barns, finding plenty of willing consumers.

6

About the middle of September we came to anchor at the tiny village of Dainville, about three kilometres out of Arras on the main road to Doullens.

The route we had followed ran parallel in its latter part with the front line, for I remember watching the star-shells soar palely into the twilight sky as we traversed the poplar- avenued road just at dusk.

By the time we reached Dainville night had fallen, but I could see that the village was not one of those derelict places fit only for troops, but passably safe for civilians as well. The church tower, certainly, reared a smashed and blunted pinnacle to the sky. One or two houses had suffered a severe punch on the bedroom storey, exposing the intimacies of their interior. One or two even, were total ruins. But, despite the regular daily arrival of a half-dozen German shells, the inhabitants had not moved away. They were loath, I suppose, to uproot themselves from old familiar scenes and abandon their homes until expelled by sheer necessity, having no other place to go.

Also, many of them were probably making a better living out of the troops than they ever made before. The thriving estaminet at the corner of the main road to Arras certainly were, for the roaring and the singing and the stamping on the sanded floor at night indicated that a swift trade was being done in bocks, vin blanc, vin rouge, and in those small but potent liqueurs.

The bouncing barmaids there were reputed to be on the free and easy side, "très, très bonne," for did they not wear Parisian high-heeled shoes? And the one or two officers who were billeted over the estaminet were considered to be uncommonly fortunate; or uncommonly enterprising to "wangle" such an opportune lodging.

I never went inside the estaminet myself, but was able to study its lively activity from over the road, as our Company Headquarters were billeted in a house exactly opposite.

When we first came to that billet in the dark, I could just dimly distinguish the red-brick facade of a typical French town house built flush with the street, its windows obscured by slatted shutters made to hook back in the day-time, its plate-glass panel let into the front door and protected by one of those florid, iron grilles, without which no French house seems to consider itself safe.

In response to our knock, French heels pattered on a tiled passage within and the door was opened by a neatly dressed, trim sort of person of that indefinable feminine age, thirty-five to forty. The flickering candle she shielded with one hand gleamed upon dank, dark hair done up on top in that bird's-nest style favoured by all middle-aged women prior to the advent of the bob and the shingle.

Madame X, however, was quite smart in a small-town way, being the widow of some defunct tradesman from Arras. Her proper name I cannot recall though I knew it well at the time; and whether her husband had been killed in the war or not, I never did know, not having enough French at that time to sustain any long conversation.

At Madame X's "Entrez, Messieurs!" we passed inside and she showed us the rooms we could use, mostly emptied of furniture. One for the officers' dining-room and office, one or two for their bedrooms, a kitchen downstairs with round French stove sticking out into the centre of the room, and an attic right at the top of the house for Bert the cook and us other hangers-on around the Mess.

"A 'ome from 'ome, ain't it?" commented Bert, glancing round the dusty attic. "Pervided a shell dont 'it the chimley an' rahse you from yer beauty sleep. Tray bong, Madam," turning to Madame and raising his voice as if speaking to a deaf person, "Tray bong cushy."

Bert Swigart, the officers' cook, was a tough East-ender with the face and figure of a pugilist. His thick lips scoffed at the world in perpetual contempt beneath a nose spread over his face like a squashed tomato, and shrewd little piggy eyes watched with cynical disdain the effect of his brief comments. Comments fired off in that clipped, staccato speech which is the true Cockney dialect as spoken from Wandsworth to Wapping, from Camberwell to Clapton.

As cook, he was self-taught, and a rotten teacher he was; but nobody dared, tell him so. Having been a lorry driver before the war he knew the City like the palm of his own hefty hand, but, like many Londoners, knew the rest of England not at all.

Five miles from the Bank in any direction comprised the hub of the universe, containing all the richest, smartest and most knowing individuals on this earth. All the rest of England, except for perhaps Brighton and Margate, was just "Dahn in the cantry" where "the Nobs" went fox-hunting and the slow-witted rustics watched the cabbages grow.

I often used to argue with him and try to impress him with descriptions of the vast industrial North, with exaggerated tales of Lancashire's power and wealth as evidenced by the huge sums of money thrown away at Blackpool during Wakes Week. But he couldn't or wouldn't swallow it, and we would go on arguing until his pots boiled over, or I had to jump to a call of "Orderly!" from the Captain.

Some of Bert's culinary processes were not strictly according to Mrs Beeton. I am sure it would have driven any economical housewife frantic to have seen him peeling potatoes. He would peel off such a thick skin that only a walnut-sized spud remained in his hand; there would have been a bigger dinner if he had boiled the skins instead.

Fish-cakes were his speciality and a treat to watch in the making; a tin of salmon and some mashed potatoes chopped together with a jack-knife and rolled into balls between grimy palms, then dropped into the boiling fat along with a little ash from a lip-clinging tab-end. When done brown they were retrieved from the fat with finger and thumb first wetted in the mouth, then dipped swiftly into the hot fat. To give Bert his due, his fish-cakes were extremely tasty, but the officers never saw the making of them.

That first night in Dainville, Crabtree ran with the usual chits while I helped Blackall fetch the officers' valises from the transport waggon.

"Come on" he said, "Give us a lift with the 'flea-bags'." So off we went through the darkened village to the transport waggon, to collect those padded sleeping-bags in which all the officer's personal belongings are rolled and, strictly on the q.t., not a few of his servant's.

"Gosh! What a weight they are," I complained, as I staggered away with the rolled-up, quilted bundle extinguishing my head and shoulders.

"Yes," grunted Blackall from under his bulging load, "Some o' these finicky blokes might think they wus goin' to the Sahth o' France, the way they fills 'em up wiv dress trahsers, silver 'air-brushes, silk pie-jamas and God knows what-all. Might be full o' perishin' cannon-balls," he sighed, as we dumped them at last in the tiled passage of our new billet.

"Got anything left over, Bert?" we inquired hopefully when the sweat had been wiped from our brows, for the slap of cards and the aroma of after-dinner coffee issuing from the Mess indicated that a meal had been consumed in our absence.

"No, ther' ain't nothin'. They've scoffed the lot." grunted Bert, picking fish-cake out of his teeth, and trying to infer by a nod that it was the officers he referred to.

"Well, the greedy bahstards!" muttered Blackall with a sweeping glance that included the officers' door, the assembled kitchen company, and almost, it seemed, Bert himself. "I 'ope it chokes 'em."

So I lay down supperless about midnight, and glad to do so, on a broken-down bed in the attic of Madame X's house. Broken-down but still a bed, the first real one I had slept on for weeks.

Madame X's house which I came to know well, as we returned to it again and again, was almost the last habitation on that side of the village. An arched gateway piercing a red-brick wall at the side, afforded a peep of a small kitchen-garden in exactly the manner of an old Dutch painting. In its middle the garden was dented by one solitary and rather ancient shellhole, looking like a small fish-pond. Apart from a few chips in the brickwork, its explosion had apparently left the house undamaged.

A footpath from the corner of the garden led up in the direction of the front line, and this path we took a few days later. Laden to the eyes with equipment, still further weighed down with Bert's pots and pans, finally extinguished by sandbags of coke, we bade "Au revoir" to Madame and departed.

• • • • •

Via the field path we went, along a road screened from "Boche" binoculars by an artificial avenue of canvas foliage, through the ruined village of Achicourt where the Battalion Office staff established themselves, onwards through tottering walls and up to as model a set of trenches as any general could wish to inspect.

In that sector where the front line straddled the railway just on the fringe of Arras, the trenches were old, well dug in and overgrown with grass and flowers. Out in front, No Man's Land was practically solid with wire. From amongst the fragmentary walls of Achicourt the trenches started, ten or twelve feet deep, winding, twisting, diverging, crossing, then ducking under the grass-grown railway track up to a deep front line. At various points on the way a wooden signpost informed you that you were, much to your surprise, in "Bond St.", "Tottenham Court Rd.", "Piccadilly" or "Shaftsbury Avenue."

In a small dug-out with roof so low that our necks were cricked by a permanent stoop, Bert fixed up a brazier, and, with his face glistening in the glow of the coke fire, did his fish-cake tricks and hashed up tins of pork and beans for the delection of the officers. The servants lay around lazily polishing tunic buttons or scraping trench dirt off their boss' boots, coughing and cursing the coke fumes, and exchanging various juicy anecdotes of their amorous adventures in pre-war days.

To the distant rattle of machine-gun fire, a coarse-faced youth from Canning Town continued his thrilling memoirs: "So we bowls aht o' the b-----g pub, dahn the b-----g road, chases the b------g tart up a b-----g alley an' runs smack into a b-----g copper wiv 'is arm rahnd another b------g 'bird'.

"Oi!" 'e 'ollers aht..." But an urgent call of "Orderly!" from the officers' adjacent dug-out robbed me of the climax to his sanguinary tale.

Every two or three hours one of us had to trot down the duck-boarded trench to Achicourt, bearing a folded chit informing Battalion Office that everything was "All quiet in 'A' Company sector;" or "Enemy seen digging east of railway. Recommend artillery strafe."

Sometimes the trip would be along the zig-zagging front line to the next Company-Commander's dug-out, requesting the loan of a bottle of whiskey until the morrow, when our Mess were expecting a new case.

The trenches being deep, the firing negligible and the "Boche" well fenced off by two-hundred yards or more of impenetrable wire, my trottings to and fro were, in the day-time, almost enjoyable. In the inky blackness of three o'clock in the morning, however, the trip to Achicourt did not feel so good.

Though I knew in the dark every turn of the trench, every break in the duck-boards, it still remained a comfort to flick on at intervals the pocket flash-lamp I always carried.

In those early hours the shadows loomed so somberly solid and the velvet night held itself so strangely still, that it seemed as if the ring of my clumping boots must echo on for miles across the battle front and inevitably rouse the enemy to reply with a salvo of fire.

"What lies beneath this deadly quiet," I would think, fingering the chit in my pocket?

"Was it a false quiet?"

The early hours, I knew, were the ones preferred for silent raids. When a dozen daring volunteers would blacken their white faces, draw muffling socks over their boots, and, armed with knives and knuckle-dusters, would steal out through a lane specially cut in the wire, into the enemy trench; there to deal out a swift and violent death, and drag hack an informative prisoner.

"Did the next shadowed bend harbour a silent raider?" I wondered; "Would the next night-rover I met turn out to be a 'square-head'?" If so I must be sure to get in the first shot or he'd certainly get me.

But travelling over the same ground next day in the cheerful sunlight, I would remind myself that at three o'clock in the morning human vitality is at its lowest ebb, and one is prone to imagine things.

The real tragedy occurred in broad day-light.

The Company Sergeant-Major, a lieutenant - I forget his name - and the jovial, popular Sergeant Downes, were making their usual tour of the front line one morning, tramping along the narrow trench in single file, when Fate suddenly interrupted their well-worn routine.

A dull "pop" from the German lines and the trio looked up to see a black speck describing an arc in the air, rapidly growing larger and larger as it drew near the end of its periphery.

They had seen it, however, a split second too late to dodge, and the rifle grenade, for such it was, dropped plump in the trench and exploded.

Rifle grenades rarely do hit the mark, and the untimely arrival of this one straight out of the blue at the precise moment of their passing, seemed like a rendezvous arranged by some inescapable Destiny. It killed outright the most cheery and lovable sergeant in the Company, sent the Lieutenant back to England with a smashed ankle, and the shaking Sergeant-Major to his dug-out for a good stiff drink.

7

In mid-October we were suddenly called away from the quiet sector of Achicourt, and rushed back into the fray of the Somme Battle, now slowing up in the autumn rains. This time we were actually carried part of the way in lorries and old London buses, the last part however being as usual, on foot.

After foot-slogging for hours through devastated country - this was all newly captured ground - the head of the column turned off the rutted road just at dusk, onto bare open land, without the vestige of a hut or tent in sight, and stopped. We had arrived at wherever it was. Before long several nice big fires were crackling merrily in the dark, and groups of men gathered round to make themselves a can of tea on the embers. The tea water, however, never had a chance to come to the boil. A droning noise overhead and the crash of two or three aerial bombs, revealed the presence of a night-flying Fokker. There was a stampede towards the fires, and in a few seconds the cheerful blaze was scattered and the red-hot embers stamped out by the cursing troops, deprived of their drink of tea.

Sky was our roof, the brown earth was our mattress, so with the others I just scraped a hole in the ground to take my hip, and lay down in my overcoat to sleep. Sleep while you can, for no one knows what the morrow with bring.

The morning light showed, spread out before us, visible from our situation on a slight hill, one of the bloodiest valleys in Europe. Standing on the high ground, I looked down onto a panorama of disrupted earth and trampled roads, and over the splintered tree-stumps of the notorious Delville Wood. In the distance, past the remnants of the village of Flers, a lowering cloud of grey smoke flickered continuously with the bursting shells.

What a water-colour effect it made, I thought, if you could only sit down and do it. Just the sort of thing a few of the famous painters had been given a free hand to do. And an officer's uniform to do it in, the lucky blighters!

The sharp crack of a rifle interrupted my reflections. A rush of feet over by an old bit of corrugated iron. "What's up?", was the general query as one man sauntered back. "Its young so-and-so shot 'is bloody self," was the reply, " 'e don't like the view."

I looked again at the view and decided that I too could have liked it better with a gilt frame round it hanging in the Leicester galleries. Unfortunately I was part of the picture this time, and had to take my place in the composition, amongst that grey smoke.

The journey up to the front line was made worse by the addition of deep mud up to the knees, for the summer weather had broken. The roads were so deeply chewed up by wheel traffic that it was easier to walk off the road than on it. Beyond Flers, the roads deteriorated into footpaths, and footpaths imperceptibly into trenches; but trenches so fragmentary that it was difficult to decide whether they were just shell-holes or not.

Never the less a bit of reserve line was found complete enough to shelter us and dumbly we rested there, waiting for something to hit us.

"Wot cher all! Got a fag on you Bert?" the speaker had just wandered along from the next bit of trench and popped his head under our tin roof. We had spent most of the last three days under a sheet of corrugated iron, roughly laid over the trench. It felt safer than it was.

"No, I aint got no fags, only this," pulling a stub end from behind his ear, "and that's got to last me 'til we git arht o' this shemozzle."

"Yes, shemozzle it is. And before we get out of it, they'll 'av us over the top again, you see if they don't"

The speaker, Collimore, was a lanky youth with glasses, typical London clerk. Tall, and so narrow chested that his ill-fitting tunic sagged across the front of him. Holding up his water-bottle to show us, he said, "See that! I've just given a bloke ten francs for it, full."

"Full o' what, beer?" somebody asked.

"No, full o' water, just plain water."

"Fancy that," said Bert. "Ten francs for a drop o' bleeding water."

"Yes! Ten francs, but what's the good of money to you in a place like this; you can't eat it. Its just bits o' dirty paper. Especially these French notes."

While we were talking, Bert had been whittling a bit of wood into splinters for fuel. He still tried to keep up a pretense of cooking for the officers, but he could do little more under the circumstances than lay a slab of bully-beef on an enamelled plate and make a drop of tea. And that often enough with stinking shell-hole water, though such a thing was expressly forbidden.

A shell falling near rattled dirt onto our tin roof, and turned the conversation into a discussion on the protective qualities of sheet iron. Collimore told about some fellow in his platoon, whose mother had sent him out an iron waistcoat, bullet-proof they were claimed to be, thinking to protect her "dear boy".

"I wouldn't wear one, not if you paid me," said Blackall emphatically, "Why, if anything hits them waistcoats it tears the iron like a sardine tin, and you die a lingering death 'stead of being put straight aht of it."

"Yes, that's right," agreed Collimore, "that's what happened to this bloke I'm telling you about. You're better without 'em"

"Ah well!" he sighed, preparing to go and glancing meaningfully at Bert's preparations for the officers, "sorry I can't stay for dinner."

"No mate," says Bert scraping some grit off a slice of bully he had dropped in the dirt, "the caviar aint none too fresh today, so buzz off!"

"Alright then! If there's nothing doing I'll drop in at the Ritz for a bite. Cheerio!" and he was gone.

"Always on the 'scrounge' that bloke" explained Bert.

"Well," remarked Blackall charitably, "he's got a long frame to fill up."

After three days of it, we thankfully handed over the sheet of corrugated iron to a relieving Company and speedily departed, though our next location was no improvement on the old. Leaving Bert and his mess-box back in Flers - the lucky devil always escaped going over the top with us - we toiled up to the front line and occupied a nasty bit of trench with one deep dug out. Deep enough to withstand anything, but all around it was shelled nearly flat.

There was a wire of sorts back to Flers, on which the signalers tapped out messages in Morse, but the thing was cut at least once an hour by the heavy shelling. The signallers spent most of their time locating the cuts and repairing them. Consequently my time was occupied in running backwards and forwards to Flers carrying the chits which kept us in touch. Crabtree had been retained by the Battalion Office to run from their end, and I was left to work from the front line end.

The way was much obscured by an undulating sea of shell-holes, and it was easy, especially at night, to walk right off the track and find yourself amongst the Germans by mistake.

Some peculiar milestones marked the route. On the open path just outside Flers there rested like a rag man's cast off, an old boot; but the foot was still in it. A bit of splintered leg-bone stuck out of it like a boot-tree. It was no worse I suppose than seeing an Egyptian mummy in the British Museum, but I used to walk well round it when I passed.

Further along a blackened, burned-out tank lay derelict. It was just here a few weeks before, that the first tanks had been tried out, and this must have been one of the first ones to burn. The charred crew were still in it, so again I passed by on the other side without examining the wreck too closely.

Just beyond the tank, the plain path petered out amongst a sea of shell-holes, and all who passes that way after dark were guided by a boulder like object which shone white and conspicuous in the moonlight. It was a dead Scotchman. His head and body were buried in the earth; likewise his legs. Only his rear portion with the kilt turned up, was left sticking out of the ground, white as an alabaster cupid.

On asking your way up to the front line you would be directed to follow this path "See? Turn sharp right by the Scotchman's arse and keep straight on. You can't miss it mate" Nor you could. On finding him and duly turning right as directed, some would touch their 'tin' hat in salute and hail him with a "Cheerio Jock" or maybe "Thanks Jock" and pass on.

Acq
The Labyrinth
Haute Avesnes
Ecurie
Roclincourt
Marœuil
Anzin
Ste Catherine
St Nicolas
St Laurent
Agnez
Duisans
Gouves
ARRAS
Montenescourt
Dainville
Blangy
Wanquetin
Achicourt
Warlus
Berneville
Beaurains
Agny
Wailly
Beaumetz
Rivière
Ficheux
Basseux
Bailleulval
Mercatel

Book 2

8

Company Sergeant-major Williams was shorter in stature than a man of his rank ought to be, according that is to "guard's" standards, not to Napoleonic. He also displayed the pinky-red complexion and the watery eye of the habitual drinker. In fact wherever you met him, no matter what the time or place, his flushed countenance seemed to betray the fact that he had just "had one".

It may of course have been partly the weathering of an unfortunate epidermis. One could never really be sure. I do know however that he was definitely not a teetotaler, because with my own eyes I have seen him what you might call "well oiled" and once or twice you could with certainty have called it "drunk". Though often near the borderline he must have known when to stop, for he was always sober enough to perform his duties.

Like many men who are fond of their tipple he was a good fellow at heart. Bullying was his job and not his inclination, for he only assumed the clipped speech of his rank when on duty.

His batman, Private Bates, was a self-possessed, dry old stick, who knew when to keep his mouth shut. When I come to recall his rather wrinkled face, it strikes me anew that though a Londoner, he must have a sprig of heather in the family somewhere.

These two got on well together, the one apparently on the verge of D.T's the other cannily plying the wet towel and the morning "corpse reviver".

One day in late October I found myself crouching down in the waist-high trenches next to the two of them, waiting for the "zero hour". A jar of rum had come up for the men, been almost knocked over in the trench by a clumsy lance-corporal, but saved in the nick of time to be justly and parsimoniously dished out, about a spoonful to each man.

The autumn sun shone warm and mellow, but as I lay there waiting for the word "go", the thought struck me that something was seriously amiss. For one thing, the company seemed frightfully shrunken in numbers. For another, the objective of the attack had only been sketchily indicated this time, and the preliminary bombardment appeared to be an unusually perfunctory affair; indeed little more than an ordinary daily "strafe".

Suddenly the idea occurred to me that what we were going to do was to be merely a feint attack, not intended to succeed, but just arranged to distract the Boche while the real push was made elsewhere.

The same idea must have occurred to Sergeant-major Williams for he had obviously got the dithers. As his batman, Bates and I crouched beside him in the shallow trench, he gazed at his wrist-watch with a glassy stare and proclaimed, "Two minutes to go".

Then, turning his whiskey-scented breath in my direction he repeated in a hoarse undertone more to himself than to me, "We shall never get out of this alive! Never! It's the finish this time". And his face as he said it took on a curious far away look, as if he were already dead and seeing visions of those others who had passed on.

It seemed like a premonition of disaster.

I watched for a moment the sweat ooze out of his raddled countenance and gather in little beads on his forehead. I turned and gazed with microscopic intensity of vision at the granules of earth a few inches from my face; examined the hairy texture of my khaki sleeve; felt the oily smoothness of my rifle-butt.

The sergeant-major moved his arm, glanced once again at his wrist watch, and I saw that the hands pointed dead on two o'clock.

Our "zero hour".

"What a pity to have to die on such a bright afternoon", I remember thinking.

Then somebody blew a whistle, and away we went.

I stumbled along, trying to keep in line as we advanced in open order; not too close to the next man, not too far away.

I could see a long undulating line of advancing troops stretching away down south, and in the distance a blue-clad line of Frenchmen also going over the top.

There was, mixed in with the general uproar, a good deal of "rat-tat-tat-ing" from somewhere. I couldn't tell quite where, as I was mainly occupied in watching the lumpy ground and trying to avoid the many shell-holes.

About half way across I looked up and about, and to my intense astonishment, found I was walking entirely alone. The whole of the advancing troops in my near vicinity had melted into the ground.

The rat-tat-tat-ing was now fully explained. Some concealed machine-gun had swept its fire along our advancing line and apparently wiped it out as clean as a wet duster on a school blackboard.

By some miracle it seemed to have missed me. The guns started traversing again just as I was thinking what a fool I should be to go on any further alone; so that decided me. I dropped down into a shell-hole out of the way of the gun for a while, and it was lucky I did so, for this time the bullets fairly whistled through my hair, so to speak, as I crouched in the shallow depression.

I could see out of the corner of my eye little spits of dust flicking off the rim of my shell-hole as the gun swept over my head, so I took good care to flatten every portion of my anatomy well down.

"What a marvel" I thought with my face pressed into the soil, "that I should be the only one missed by that deadly machine-gun. There must have been a blank or a misfire or something just as it pointed in my direction".

It soon became evident that any further movement was impossible. Taking a cautious look round I discovered that I had been mistaken after all in thinking that I was the only one to escape untouched. A few others like myself also appeared to have been miraculously preserved and were now marooned in shell-holes half way across no-mans-land, unable to dash forward, or even backwards to our own trench; unable even to stir a head without attracting instant fire from that "Boche" machine-gun.

As it happened we were far safer where we were; for looking back I could see a tremendous amount of heavy stuff bursting along our old starting line, throwing huge columns of dirt high into the air.

The only sensible thing to do now was to stay in the shell-hole until darkness set in, filling in the time until then by taking pot-shots at the Germans, who could be seen walking about in the open. Keep 'em on the jump so that they wouldn't be tempted to pay us a visit. Several rifle-cracks from nearby shell-holes told me that others were also doing the same thing.

I wished there had been somebody else in the same hole with me, just for company; but there I was, just like a Bairnsfather cartoon of "Old Bill" in his "better 'ole".

As the afternoon wore on the "Boche" ceased their bobbing about in the open and I had nothing to do but wait. Wait and watch the October sunlight gild the roofs and spires of distant Bapaume; a town within our sight but as yet beyond our grasp.

I looked at my watch to see how much longer I must wait for darkness, and then I suddenly remembered; it was Saturday afternoon! Half holiday!

Father would be home from the works, pottering about the garden probably, Alice, my sister would be popping off to the lending library to change her books for Sunday. I wondered what they would be having for tea; tinned pears probably, they often had them on a Saturday; or maybe stewed rhubarb, there was a huge plant of it in the garden. No! Wrong time of year for rhubarb.

Funny to think of them all sitting there this very minute, eating thin bread and butter, absolutely unaware of the tough spot I was in. This, I supposed, must be the point in the story where "his whole life flashes before him".

Towards the end of October it gets dark fairly early.

"The days are drawing in," it was a trite remark they usually made at home, "we shall have to be lighting up for tea."

So at last the light faded, and before long it was dark enough for me to crawl out of the shell-hole unobserved. I moved along in a stooping attitude to avoid silhouetting myself against the skyline, but I had gone no more than a few yards before I ran into a crowd of figures loping along in the same monkey-like fashion, all making for our own lines. Almost the first couple I recognised in the dark, were the Sergeant-major and Bates.

"Hullo Clayton," he said with a grin, "You alright too! That's good! We'll soon be out of it now" and with that they both passed on into the darkness.

Many of the crowd had been hit by the machine-gun fire. Some were not seriously hurt, some could just stagger along, some were crawling along, a few were being carried in on the backs of their comrades, and many were left to be collected by the Red Cross stretcher-bearers, who had begun to appear out of the night. The rest were beyond collection.

I heard somebody moaning to be given a drink of water, and somebody else saying "No! Don't give 'im no water. The poor blighters been 'it in the stomach. Water 'll kill 'im".

Looking for trenches which were no longer there, having been flattened out by those big shells I had seen, I almost fell down the opening of our old deep dugout. It was crammed full of wounded who were unable to walk, sitting or lying all the way down the twenty-odd steps, awaiting the overworked stretcher-bearers. New regiments had been rushed up to replace us, so all who could walk were told to "shoot off back to Flers" as soon as they liked; and nobody needed telling twice.

Knowing the way better than most, I went off at the head of a string of the halt and the lame; guiding them along the tortuous path and leaving behind for the last time, the dead Scotchman, the derelict tank, and the boot with the foot still in it.

In Flers, the Colonel and Headquarters staff were established in a series of caves dug into a bank of earth, looking just like a row of rabbit holes in a bank-side. When the shells began to fall they all popped into the holes, and when they stopped, they all popped out again. Nearby, some old trenches similarly honey-combed with holes of varying sizes, housed quite a large number of individuals such as signallers, cooks, transport drivers, Battalion Office clerks, and many others whose duties were such that they were never required to go over the top.

This time however, they had had a very hot time. Bert had been one of the party and according to his blasphemous account of the incident, they had done heroic work in dragging water-carts and stores up the deeply rutted road, while shells fell thick and fast all around them.

As we jaded remnants of the company reached Flers we were welcomed by the sight of Sergeant-major Saunders, that Tartar of a regimental, actually unbending for a moment. He thrust a tin cup into my hand, slapped me on the shoulder and snapped out, "Drink that up my boy! It'll do you good!" The cup was more than half full of neat rum, probably more in a single cup than I had drunk in all my life before.

I swigged it up in one hurried gulp, and gasping for breath moved away; while he, dipping the cup again in the pail of rum at his feet, served the rest in like manner.

I just had time to stagger along to an old bit of trench and roll into a "funk hole" in the side of it before the rum took effect, and I knew no more until nearly noon of the following day.

With that fiasco of an attack our work was done for a while, and we moved out to recuperate and count the missing. Passing between the splintered trunks of Delville Wood, hurrying round its "Suicide Corner" before anything dropped on us, we came to rest in the open country near Trones Wood. In this busy back area, amongst the big guns firing at their invisible targets, the roll was called.

More than half of my Company was found to have disappeared. Of those who had actually gone over the top only about twenty remained. The Company commander, Captain Tite, still lived to conduct affairs with his usual unruffled equanimity, but two or three Lieutenants had "Gone West", including Blackall's boss.

Collimore's tall lanky figure was also conspicuous by its absence and we feared he was "out for the count". Fortunately he turned up again three or four weeks later, beaming through his thick spectacles.

"Where've you been, Colly boy?" he was asked, "We thought you was shoving daisies up."

"No Mate. Not this time. A bit of shrapnel stuck in my arm and I've been back in a base hospital with it. Had a posh time back there pottering about with bandages, helping to dish out the grub, emptying the old doings, and what-not".

"Lucky swine!" says Bert, "and there we been using black edged snot-rags for you, and 'oping you was finding the weather cool".

As for Sergeant-major Williams, he was strutting about with his pink face wreathed in smiles, very pleased with himself. It seems he had persuaded one of the few living officers to bear witness that he and Bates had done great things that Saturday afternoon, and to put their names forward for some kind of decoration.

I had seen them both start and I had seen them return; what they did in the meantime I don't know, but the recommendation was passed through, approved on high, and in due course the awards were handed out. For Bates, a Military Medal, and for the Sergeant-major, a D.C.M. So much for his premonition!

9

The battalion which wended its way along the St. Pol road towards Arras in November was a refreshed and strengthened unit. After our losses on the Somme the numbers were brought up to strength again with fresh recruits from England.

New faces soon drove into oblivion the memory of those others dead and gone; and with the new faces came new tunes from the recent London shows as well as new slang words from the training camps. Songs from the "Bing Boys" were hummed and whistled in the billets, the new catchy tune "Broken Doll" quickly became repeated ad nauseam and "Jerry", the new slang word for the Germans, caught on. Up to then we had always called them "Boche".

We who had been out since July were now "Old Sweats". The few odd ones like Bert who were the relics of still earlier times, were regarded almost as encrusted museum pieces from the bow and arrow days. Our Air Force had the upper hand of the Germans, and it was generally considered that now we had, in vulgar parlance, "got them by the short hairs".

After a long day's march our battalion approached the ancient town of Arras. A town with a long and picturesque history, it was famous in the Middle Ages for the manufacture of the tapestry hangings which bear its name, and used to clothe in the days of chivalry, the walls of every medieval castle. How many times in history have the spies and murderers concealed their villainous persons behind the arras?

If the story of the town could have been woven into one of those tapestries, what a pattern of unexampled richness would appear. Great names of long dead emperors and generals embroidered over a background of siege and fire, alliance and peace treaty, while cutting across the fabric would run the dread name of Citizen Robespierre, native of Arras.

The wealthy burghers of the past built solidly and carved richly, and in spite of the modern high explosives much of it still remained in 1916, though sadly battered. Practically the whole of the town was in our hands, the German line passing through the outer suburb of Blangy, and though the normal population had been evacuated, a few daring civilians still remained behind to guard their possessions or to trade with the troops.

As we entered the town for the first time by the old Porte de Baudimont, the tramp of our army boots echoed under the stone arch of the Porte and rang on the cobbles of the narrow main street. That street which, cutting straight through the heart of the town, begins as the Rue de Baudiment and ends up at the station as the Rue de Gambetta.

This was the first French town of any size that I had entered, apart from Boulogne; so I looked with interest at the time-rounded stones and at the more recent shop fronts, now securely shuttered, which modern progress had built into the old facades.

The trade names over the shops were intriguing too when painted up in French. Charcuterie, Boulangerie, Boucherie, au Bon Marche, met the eye.

Most of the owners of these businesses however, had long since closed their shutters, sealed the wine cellar door with official stamp, locked the shop for the last time and departed with a sinking heart.

It was dark by the time our Company came to a halt in the Rue de Gambetta, and the occasional star shells soaring somewhere behind the station told us that "Jerry" was not far away. At the "Company dismiss" I followed the rest of the officer's mess gang to our billet for the night.

We turned off the Rue de Gambetta, down a narrow street to the left, Rue St. Gery I think it was called, stopped a few yards along it, and mounting two or three steps, entered the shop door of a boulangerie. Behind the baker's counter inside, Bert was just chucking his pack down on the floor, running his eye over the fixtures and looking round for a cooking stove on which to get to work.

"Not a bad kip here," he commented, "This'll do me for duration."

I also dropped my pack on the floor but was unable to explore the house for a while, being sent off almost immediately by the captain, with some message or other. By the time I had located the billets of the Sergeant-major and of the four platoons of men, and delivered the message, the evening was well advanced.

The baker's house in the Rue St. Gery was both high and deep. Not only did it tower up several stories, but it also buried itself in the ground to a depth of three cellars, one underneath the other. When we subsequently explored them, we found them as solidly built as cells in the Bastille, which they resembled, and in the bottom cellar of all which was reached through a square hole in the wall of the second cellar, the wily baker had hidden his store of logs.

We supposed he must have used these logs for firing his ovens, situated in the first cellar.

The ground-floor rooms had been cleared of furniture, probably used for fuel by previous troops, and when I returned that first night I found the others had not been idle. They had managed to find some of the baker's logs, and had built up on the huge hearth of the main salon downstairs, the biggest fire I have ever seen inside a house.

Bert said, "Go outside somebody and 'ave a dekko at the chimney. We'll 'ave the ruddy Jerries sending us a billy doox if they see that blaze."

Somebody went out to look, but nothing showed outside, so another log was thrown on and we settled ourselves to sleep on the hard floor round the big blaze, while the officers occupied what beds were still left in the furnished rooms upstairs.

The personnel of the Company's officers had changed considerably of late. The unassuming but quietly efficient Captain Tite still commanded the Company. He was reputed to be in civil life, a tea planter from Ceylon. The four platoons were now officered by lieutenants Backlake, Scollick, "Tubby" Edwards and Maude.

Backlake and Scollick, to do them no discredit, were just a couple of ordinary young coves, might have been secondary school teachers or bank clerks.

Lieutenant Edwards, as his nick-name implied, was rather short and tubby, and a little older than the others. He was essentially of a shy and reserved nature, apt to stutter a little if embarrassed, and meticulously conscientious in performing any task allotted to him. He differed from the rest in that he could speak extremely fluent French, having been in some kind of business in northern France before the war.

I remember one occasion on which a stubborn farm labourer refused to move his hay cart out of the way of our marching column, and the expression on the fellow's face, which was transformed into a picture of rustic surprise as Tubby turned round and blasted away at him in his own patois.

Yes, Tubby was a useful man.

Lieutenant Maude was the infant of the outfit. Pathetically young, his slender fragile build, his fair hair and inability to grow anything on the upper lip, made him seem a mere schoolboy, which indeed he was. He was given No.4 platoon to command, and those tough hard-boiled old sweats, old enough to be his father, took to him instantly and protected him from the many dangers of trench life, so far as was possible.

I once heard a sergeant reprove a lance-corporal for calling him "Maudie".

"Mister Maude to you, you lousy so-and-so, or I'll knock yer blinking teef 'arht" See!"

He drilled his platoon in a cultured, school cadet-corps voice, straining to achieve a loud authoritative shout. And those rough devils listened for it and jumped to it like lightning, "just to please the kid" as they said.

He would speak proudly of "my men" and when at dinner in the mess the Captain congratulated him on the smartness of his platoon, he was boyishly delighted.

There was however another side to the picture. He would question closely the other officers about their over-the-top experiences, listening avidly to their most casual replies. A strained expression and a nervous bravado told the story of one who had to force himself to appear unafraid. He was one of those physically weak but imaginative people who instinctively withdraw from displays of crude force, and it was probably only the greater fear of disgracing his officer's uniform that gave him strength to face the dangers.

Which gives one cause to reflect that the greatest courage after all, is to go on when you are frightened. Any fool can be brave who does not stop to think.

Changes too had been made amongst us lesser fry below the salt. The dapper little Crabtree had been promoted to a bicycle, and running for the Battalion office instead of for A. Company; so I lost my partner. His place was taken by a hefty-shouldered Lancashire man, an ex-solicitor's clerk from Manchester, named Harry Arnold.

Arnold was a good "scrounger", always ready to do a bit of unofficial foraging, and our first job when we had a spare moment, was to investigate the houses adjoining our boulangerie.

The charm of living in a bombarded town like Arras, lay for us in the fact that all the normal inhabitants had not only gone, but gone in a deuce of a hurry. They had just grabbed the family stocking from under the loose board, slung their Sunday best into a suitcase, locked the wine cellar door, and shot off:

Leaving as often as not, the coffee cups still on the breakfast table and the bedclothes all disordered just as they jumped out at the crack of the first shell over the town.

The doors of the houses were all locked of course, except those commandeered for billets, and the wine cellars were all sealed with a round blob of wax, and impressed with the official stamp by the gendarmerie.

To break those seals was to commit the serious crime of looting.

As it happened the breaking-in was often accomplished by German shelling, so it could hardly be classed as a crime if one strayed through a hole in a wall, maybe enlarging the hole a little at the same time. The house next door to us however, appeared to be quite undamaged, so we climbed up the stairs to the top of our own house and examined it by looking out of our attic window across the leads. The ancient dormer window of the next door attic faced us only about ten feet away, and it was the work of but a moment to scramble across the leads, lever open the window, and climb through.

The first room we entered below the attic stairs was a bedroom. A woman's bedroom too by the look of the many articles of feminine apparel strewn about. The lace-trimmed nightdress thrown hastily across a gilded chair and the bottles of lotion, scent, hair wash and God-knows-what standing on one of those Frenchy-looking commodes.

On the mantelpiece we found one of those humorously vulgar little china figures sitting on a little china pot, which made us guffaw. French pottery humour tends rather to chamber pots with eyes painted at the bottom, but nobody seems to mind

It seemed as if a shell must have burst on the roof at some time, for the plaster had been shaken loose from the ceiling and fallen in a big pancake, flat across the elaborately carved bed. Everything in the room was covered with plaster-dust and debris.

"Gosh!" said Arnold, looking up at the ceiling, "I bet that woke her up with a start, if she was there when it happened. Come on let's go downstairs and see if the cellar's intact."

Arnold always had a nose for bottles, and as there was nothing upstairs that we could use, down below we went.

It appeared that the wine cellar door was in a tiny courtyard at the back, and securely locked. Arnold was for breaking a hole in it with a chunk of wood or something, but I reminded him that the courtyard was overlooked and in any case it wouldn't do to make a noise, so he reluctantly abandoned the idea and we entered the house again.

In the tiled passage, behind the iron grilled and locked front door, we found a bicycle in good condition.

"That's the very thing for us" he said, "We can ride it in turns instead of foot slogging all the way. Why, dammit! Battalion orderlies 'ave bikes, why shouldn't we?"

I didn't think we should be able to use it much, but he seemed set on having it, so I didn't bother to disagree.

"The front door's locked "I pointed out, "We shall have to get it through the attic, the way we came."

After a great deal of trouble we got the bicycle up the dark winding staircase as far as the attic. It would only just go through the square dormer-window by holding it sideways, so with much sweating and swearing we had just managed to get it half way out, when a loud banging on the front door echoed through the empty house.

"It's the ruddy police" said Arnold, "Let's get it through quick, before they get up here!"

We tussled feverishly with the bike and after what seemed an age we got it out on the leads; another frantic tussle and at last it was through our own dormer-window. Downstairs with it we rushed almost falling down headlong in our haste, through the lower rooms, now empty of officers, thank the Lord, and down the stone cellar steps. Down into the depths of that third cellar we took it, and hid it under the baker's logs.

With intense relief we returned to ground floor level, bathed in perspiration from our exertions, and just in time to see a couple of French gendarmes come out of the next house, locking the door behind them.

"Some blasted Froggie must 'av seen us in that courtyard and given 'em the tip" commented Arnold.

"An' all for a perishing bike" added Bert, giving a stir to the pan of stew on the stove. "Lumme! Why don't you blokes bust a cellar open sometimes? Do a lot more good to your thirsty pals."

Strange to relate I had never up to then learnt to ride a bicycle, so I left it to Arnold. After filing off the registration number, for all cyclists are licensed in France, he used it for three or four weeks, until finally it was stolen from him by some other "scrounger" anxious to give his feet a rest.

10

The night before we left the boulangerie to go up into the front line, I felt very seedy. Whether it was the 'flu coming on or a touch of trench fever, I didn't know and was feeling too groggy to care.

I think it was Blackall who suggested that a half bottle of red wine drunk very hot was a marvelous cure for the 'flu. Luckily the red wine was to hand, in fact it was running like water just at that moment. Someone had discovered a cellar nearby and had also found a way of loosening the wax seal without breaking it, by slipping a heated knife underneath and easing it off the wood. Picking the lock was easy after that. As easy as the replacing of the seal after the bottles had been passed up.

The wines which we poured out like so much ginger beer, knocking off the tops of the bottles for lack of a corkscrew, might have been for all we knew, epicurean nectars of the choicest vintage. Delicate clarets, sparkling burgundies or fine old crusted ports, they were all one to us, just "red ink".

Bert declared emphatically, spitting out a mouthful on the floor, that for him "anybody could 'ave this vin blanc and vin rouge"; he'd rather "blow the froth off a nice glarss o' pig's ear, any day o' the week".

I filled up my enamelled water bottle with red wine of some kind, ready to take up the trenches in the morning, and drank about half a bottle-full, scalding hot, before laying down in a corner to sleep.

Apparently the prescription was an excellent one, for I felt very much better the next morning, and took my place with the Company with nothing worse than a fat head, as they filed up the Rue de Gambetta and moved towards the front line.

We crossed over the trainless railway line near the iron skeleton of the station, with its hundreds of panes of glass long since shattered by the tattoo of machine-gun bullets which played on it daily, and picked our way in single file along the streets of crumbling houses.

This was the manufacturing district of Arras, and our bit of line turned out to be a length of trench which wormed its way through the cellars and back yards of working-class houses, round a couple of battered factory boilers with their steam pipes all twisted up like iron macaroni, and into the basement of the factory itself.

Directions were puzzling. The trench would take a sudden turn through the relic of a doorway into a bit of cellar, then up a step or two and out through another doorway, twist round a lot of rusty machinery, to dive suddenly through a hole in the factory wall to another bit of cellar.

It was one of those hush-hush places, with the Boche entrenched only a few yards away, in some places only a few feet, and everybody being exhorted to speak only in whispers if they wished to live a long life. At certain points, only the brick wall of the factory divided us, and by listening quietly a low murmur of guttural conversation and a clinking of accoutrements could be heard.

It was exactly like one of those suburban houses where you can hear when the man next door taps his pipe out on the hearth, or his wife pokes the fire, or their alarm clock wakes you half an hour before your own is due to go off.

On our side of the brick wall there still stood the stump of the old factory chimney, which made for us a really valuable observation post. The observers used to climb up a rope ladder inside, and squint down into the enemy trenches through holes that had been bored in the brickwork.

In spite of the nearness of Jerry, or perhaps because of it, the line was very quiet. An occasional sniper's bullet would whine past your ear to ping against the rusty old boiler, and remind you to keep your head down; or a rifle grenade would come lobbing over and explode, just to prove as it were that the war was still on and that your life was still liable to be cut short.

Our first sojourn in Arras was brief. Just in and out the line once or twice and then away we went. As usual nobody knew where we were bound for; whether it was up north or down south or just behind the lines a little way, in reserve. Anyway, it was back out of reach of shell-fire, so that was something to the good.

The weather had turned very cold, the ground froze as hard as iron, making trench digging slow work, and the wind had started to whistle through the cracks in those barns, in spite of the newspaper stuffed into them.

Once again we were away from the devastated areas, tramping the tree-lined roads of rural Picardy, sleeping in barns, drinking vin blanc in village estaminets, or little cups of bitter coffee in farm kitchens. Dozens of remote hamlets and villages with curious names tolerated us for a short time, offering bread and eggs, wine and spirits, omelets and cafe noir, in exchange for dirty five-franc notes. Places with names like Blavincourt, Warlus, Habarcq, Avesnes-le-Comte – quite a town this, and pronounced "Avey-ler-Com", Noyellette, Wailly, Wanquentin, and a score of others, knew us for a night or perhaps two, then on again.

The cold wind blowing across the open fields between villages, often stiffened the hand that carried the rifle, and when sergeant yelled "Platoon 'tshun! Slo-pe umps!" you had to be careful not to let it slip through frozen fingers.

Just before Christmas, 1916, we occupied a tiny village, the name of which has entirely escaped my memory. All I can remember about its location is the feeling of being away from the major roads, of being right off the map for the time being and buried in the country. And there we stayed for about six weeks, right over Christmas.

It was a very small village indeed, consisting chiefly of one main road lined on both sides for about a mile with the usual ramshackle dwellings; you couldn't exactly call them farms, though they were all set back behind a manurey-smelling courtyard and approached through an arched gateway fronting the road. There was also a crossroad of lesser importance and three or four odd bits of lane that seemed, like one's appendix, to lead nowhere. So few were the houses, that our battalion with its four companies of men filled every available barn, and our officers every farmhouse billet.

Everyone agreed that "this was too cushy a thing to last long", and very likely some disagreeable purpose lay behind the quiet interlude. As the days rolled on the purpose became plain. We were being drilled and marched and coached anew in bomb-throwing, in preparation for some big new offensive they were planning for the spring.

Commented Bert one evening as three or four of us sat round the red-hot French stove in the farmhouse kitchen, "Another bloody Somme push for us next year."

It was turning out a hard winter, the frost glistened on the window panes and rimed even the straw in the steaming manure-pit outside, making the hot stove in the kitchen doubly welcome.

"Yes" added Blackall, "another bloody push for us. I wonder how many of us 'll be sitting round this 'ere stove next Christmas."

"Well I hope I sha'nt be here for one" observed Arnold, "I'm fed up to the back teeth already."

"Fed up to the back teeth with my Yorkshire pudden, you big boozer", countered Bert. "You wait 'til you bin 'ahrt as long as me an' Blackall 'ere before your start grousing."

"Ow long 'ave you bin 'ahrt now, Bert?" queried Blackall, "Since 1915 'aint yer?

Bert spat meditatively at the hot stove before replying, watched it sizzle to a little dancing drop, and rejoined,

"Yes mate, since 1915, and I aint been 'ome on leave since we was up at Hulluch. Thirteen blasted months without a peep at the old Commercial Road. 'Ows that for doing yer bit, you Derby conscript?" This last being a dig at Arnold, though he was really no Derby man.

"Ah well" I added, "perhaps you'll touch lucky this Christmas, I heard somebody say they'd started leave again, and one or two have already gone from D. Company."

The discussion was interrupted by a call from the officer's mess in the adjoining room, the farmer's best parlour, where the five of them having finished dinner had brought out the glasses and the Johnny Walker, and were just making up a four for bridge.

Blackall being the mess-waiter, answered the call and as he returned a burst of laughter floated out through the parlour door.

"They seem to be enjoying themselves" observed Arnold.

"They're pulling Tubby's leg" replied Blackall. "He's Mess President this week and they're kidding him for trying to keep the whiskey bills down."

Lieutenant Edwards was not a wealthy man, and when it was his turn to be Mess President, this is to buy all the provisions for the five of them, he would try to do it as economically as he could, being a careful soul.

A profligate Mess President could easily embarrass the poorer officers by a too lavish expenditure. "Hang the expense, we'll soon be dead." was a motto often adopted by many Company Messes. And the poor ones sometimes had quite a job to keep up the pace.

"'Ow abaht a game o' pontoon" suggested Bert, bringing out a pack of greasy cards and looking round the group.

"Alright" agreed Blackall, Arnold and young Bill Dewer, Scollick's servant and newcomer to the mess.

"Deal 'em out then" said Blackall, bringing our only two candles on to the table.

“Leave me out of it this time” I said, “I don’t play cards much.”

“Don’t smoke, don’t drink, don’t gamble; you’re missing an ‘ell-ov-a-lot o’ fun, young ‘un!” replied Bert.

“Well! Come on you blokes, if you don’t speculate, you don’t accumulate!

Cut the cards somebody!”

11

Leaving them to their game of pontoon, I went out into the frosty night. Following the brick path around the frozen manure-pit, I stopped and turned under the arched gateway to look back at the moonlit courtyard, and at the ramshackle farm-house with its shuttered windows. The warm light escaping into the blue-grey night through the cracks of the shutters, was almost too like a colour print to be real.

Slipping through a little wicket in the heavy wooden door, I turned down the road for a few yards and then through a similar wicket leading into an almost identical farmyard.

This time instead of going up to the house, I made for the rambling old granary which stretched along the gateway side of the yard, facing the house. This granary was the present abode of my platoon with whom I now made my bed, as there was little reason in this remote village for hanging around the mess waiting for messages.

Pushing aside the brown tattered blanket which hung over the entrance, I stepped over the threshold. Two rows of wire netting beds ranged the walls, and the three or four flickering candles threw up into the hollow roof a grotesque shadow pattern of the supporting beams.

Wreathed in the smoke from cheap "gaspers", a crowd of men sat around on the beds or squatted on the floor, all perfectly silent, except for one man in the middle who, seated on a box, intoned monotonously a series of numbers which he read from a paper.

"Twenty nine… Forty seven… Seventeen… Sixty-five… he went on, reading slowly, Forty-one… Legs-eleven… Eighty five… Clickety-click… Twenty two… Coming of age… Kelly's eye..."

As fast as he called them out the crowd were busily marking off the numbers on a card each held up to the dim light.

Suddenly the concentration of the men and the recital of the string of numbers was rudely shattered by one man, who jumping up vociferated, "Housey House!" Here y'are, house full."

"Righto! 'And yer card up, mate" replied the man who had been intoning the numbers. After a careful check over, the owner of the full card was paid out with a handful of small change, and the game went on.

The game of "House" was a very mild gamble, supposed to be the only one officially permitted by the King's Regulations. The players bought for a few pence, cards on which were printed a series of numbers. The money thus collected being paid out again to the holder of the first card to be completed, less of course a percentage which the organiser deducted for his trouble.

As the numbers were called out, it was the custom to substitute some allusive phrase or alliteration which gave an amusing twist to the intended number.

Sixty-six for instance, was always 'clickety-click'. Number one, was 'Kelly's eye'. One hundred, was 'Top o' the house'; and nine was 'Medicine and Duty', a reference to the doctor's number nine pill which was ten times as rapid and effective as castor-oil.

As I sat back on my bed unrolling my puttees in preparation for the night, the enterprising organiser started a fresh game by calling out, "Come on my lucky lads, just time for one more game. Who says a card! Who says a lucky card! Roll up for a lucky card!"

Having sold sufficient cards, he started the ball rolling once more by calling out, "Eyes down! Look in!" upon which all heads bent down to peruse the new cards, and the tale of numbers rolled monotonously on.

The weather continued to get colder and colder. Snow fell gently, covering the countryside with a white mantle, also drifting through the great holes and cracks in our granary walls so that I awoke one morning to find my blanket half covered with snow.

We used to wash our shirts in the farmyard on a trestle table, laying them on the board and scrubbing vigorously with a stiff brush, the water too freezing cold to lather properly. I conceived the idea of leaving mine hanging out all night in the intense cold, so that the livestock which infested the flannel would catch a severe chill, and perhaps die.

The attempt was unsuccessful however as I feared it would be, for though the shirt froze as stiff as a sheet of glass, it returned to life as itchy as ever when warmed up again on my back.

Christmas day arrived; and with it a twenty-four hours respite from the sickening boredom of the everlasting drill. A slap-up dinner with real plum pudding, served up on the granary floor as usual of course, but plenty of it. The day marred only by Arnold getting stinking drunk on a fancy bottle of anisette he had carried from Arras, and being disgustingly sick all over my overcoat.

Anisette is a strong liqueur apparently made from aniseed, for the vile smell of that aromatic seed lingered in my overcoat for days, reminding me of the aniseed balls we used to suck as children.

Arnold was not by any means the only one to imbibe too freely of the Christmas spirit, for what better excuse can a toper have than Christmas! There positively isn't a better! By midday, Company Sergt. Major Williams also had acquired a considerable stagger in his walk and a hiccup in his speech, and by evening he had lost all power to walk at all.

The estaminets, I believe there were only two in the village, supplied bocks, vins blanc and liqueurs to those who could squeeze through the door and elbow a place up to the zinc counter. Amongst the glittering bottles behind the counter, Madame and family, overwhelmed by the unprecedented rush of business, beamed and nodded to all and sundry, their faces shining with the heat, and the smoke, and the good business they were doing.

Collimore and I being non-drinkers, patronised an equally crowded farm kitchen, where an elderly Madame in old fashioned black alpaca, dispensed little cups of black coffee at one franc fifty a time, made very sweet with oblong pieces of sugar.

While we all sat around the low beamed kitchen, she kept a big black pan of the coffee perpetually bubbling on the stove, filling the cups with a tin scoop and throwing a fresh handful of chicory and coffee in the pan from time to time.

The short December afternoon closed in, and as we betook ourselves back we met the mess orderlies staggering along to the various barns and billets with the big dixies of tea, yelling "Tea up!" as they dumped it under the archway. Even at home nobody wants tea on Christmas day, and the lack of enthusiasm shown for it here was in no way exceptional. The mess orderlies need hardly have troubled to fetch it, for the dixies were left standing out in the cold, still half full.

The evening was topped off with a big Battalion concert party and general sing-song, held in the largest barn in the village. The dapper Colonel of the Battalion with all his officers, fresh - very fresh - from their 7p.m. Christmas dinner, occupied the 'stalls' and laughed uproariously at the sly wit and very broad jokes of the amateur performers.

The buffoonery of three characters named respectively Freeman, Hardy and Willis, evoked roars of laughter, while the appearance of a well known corporal made up as Mademoiselle from Armentières called forth from the packed audience, whistles, lewd catcalls, the sound of smacking kisses, and calls of "show a leg there, show a leg!"

The audience rapidly achieved that state of well-oiled hilarity reached only in the East End variety halls on a Saturday night, when the fat comedienne has worked them up to such a pitch that the stalest of gags lifts the roof, and the slightest of winks rocks the house.

Needless to say there was no difficulty about getting them to sing, the greatest difficulty being to stop the encores so that the next act could go on. The roof timbers trembled and creaked to the tunes of "Good-bye-ee!", "The Army of To-days's All Right", "If You Were the Only Girl in the World", and of course "Another Little Drink wouldn't do us any Harm".

When all the show was over and the last incapable had been guided safely to his billet, when the lousy brown blankets had enveloped their occupants and the bugles had echoed their last call of 'lights out' over the sleeping village, Collimore rolled himself up in his blanket, snuffed the candle with his fingers and remarked to me, "Not such a dusty Christmas after all. Pity the folks at home don't know where we are and how we're doing."

"Yes," I said, "my folks would be having a happier Christmas if they knew we were out of harm's way for a little while."

"Yes, for ju-st a little whi-ile" he added, repeating the words of a popular song as he buried his face under the blanket.

12

The Commanding Officer of the Battalion, Lieutenant-colonel "Dolly" Cooper, seemed at first glance to have been aptly named. A dapper little man, sallow complexion, black haired like a Mexican, always perfectly dressed, he had the air of having lived most of his forty-odd years in Mayfair drawing rooms, or in one of those vast Palladian country houses complete with stables, topiary gardens and deer park.

One felt that an abyss divided his mode of life from that of the 'Gor blimey' mob he commanded. The delicate shade of his breeches alone betokened a taste for the elegant and precious graces of life, their subtle tint more akin to a ripe peach than a vulgar khaki.

The coarse cloth which covered the manly form of the common soldier was just khaki, plain khaki. A nasty greenery-yellery colour, bilious enough to turn a cow sick. Still! There it was: the regulation colour, and we had to take it.

Officers, on the other hand, held the privilege, if it could be called such, of buying their own clothes. Consequently, the variations played on the theme of khaki were diverse and subtle in the extreme, ranging from a soft canary-yellow, through more normal khakis, up to a delicate maiden's blush.

Staff officers especially were often partial to fancy variations and noted for a broad-minded interpretation of the word khaki.

But somehow, with "Dolly" Cooper, the lie was given to those delectable breeches by the sharp tilt of his tin hat, the darting glance of his black eyes and his quick, hopping gait, "like a blinking sparrer" as Bert described it. The "Dolly" exterior was a thin shell which covered a daring and fearless spirit*, a shrewd judgement, and a sharp eye for any slackness of discipline or relaxation of effort.

*Note. As was amply proved by the mode of his death during the dark days of March, 1918. He was killed while leading the battalion in an attempt to stem the flood of the great German break-through, and awarded a posthumous V.C.

If he had a fault, and to my mind it is a common fault amongst those who have never known anything but riches, it lay in a rather cold, superior detachment from the lower orders of life. You felt that he had never been east of Aldgate Pump, except perhaps in a swift car on the way to some Essex country house.

I remember an occasion just after one of our Somme attacks, when he addressed the troops. We were lined up in the shell-torn main street of Achicourt at the time, standing stiffly to attention, rifles at the slope, not daring to flicker an eyelid for fear the eagle eye of the Regimental Sergt.-major should spot a tremor, when "Dolly" Cooper began his oration.

Slapping his dandy breeches with a small cane, he began in a slow, distance piercing shout, throwing his light voice down the long ranks like a ventriloquist.

"My men! - I - want - to - tell - you -" turning to throw his voice the other way, "I - want - to - tell - you - all, that - last - weekend - I - was - in - London - "

"The lucky bastard" muttered the man next to me out of the side of his mouth, "an' I 'aint bin 'ome for a ruddy twelvemonth."

"I - was - in - London" continued 'Dolly', "and - when I told them of your - ah - achievements out he-ah, - they told me to tell you that - ah - London - is - proud - of - you. Delighted with your - ah - success. Thrilled with your - ah - achievements. Yes, - London is proud of you. Proud of you. Now - that is a very fine compliment to pay - ah - very fine indeed, - but - I must remind you that you still have plenty to do before the - ah - Boche is - ah - vanquished. And I want you to - ah - go to it with renewed - ah - energy, - and - ah - zeal, - knowing that London is - ah - watching you, and that London is - ah - proud of you. Don't let them down!"

As the speech concluded, a spate of crisp orders broke out, we relaxed our tension, and my neighbour of the sotto voice twisted his mouth once again and muttered, "He-ah! He-ah!"

During our six weeks out of the firing line, the battalion under 'Dolly' Cooper's energetic direction, was being knocked into shape again ready for big operations in the New Year.

He was putting the younger officers through their paces too, particularly the new lieutenants and second-lieuts who had joined us since the Somme.

This became evident one morning when Second-lieutenant Scollick took me aside in the mess and observed quietly, "You can draw a bit, can't you, Clayton?"

"Yes sir, I can draw a bit," says I brightly, thinking there had been an inquiry for a draughtsman somewhere back in a base camp, and I was going to be offered the job and get out of all the muck and the slaughter. My rosy picture quickly faded however, as he continued with a look of relief on his face, at my claim to skill with the pencil.

"Good! Splendid! That's fine!" he said. "Now, I can't draw for toffee, and I've got to do a map of this village for the colonel, just as an exercise you know, showing all the billets, stores, headquarters, incinerators, and what-nots; do you think you can do it for me?"

"Yes sir," I replied, "I can do that alright, if you can give me a little time off to look over the place."

"Righto! Clayton, I'll fix it with Captain Tite so that you need not attend parades for a couple of days." with a reassuring nod, "That'll be alright, won't it?"

"Yes sir, thank you very much." And bang goes my hope of a base job, I thought. Just like the army! They've got artists digging trenches and navvies drawing maps; they make clerks into tailors, tailors into plumbers and plumbers into clerks again.

During the next two days I wandered all over the village, up every by-lane, round every house barn or shed, even into every pig-sty perchance it might be somebody's billet; recording here a barn for twenty men; there, the quartermaster's stores; somewhere else, a cookhouse; over in that field, two latrines and an incinerator.

In fact, I thoroughly enjoyed putting my skill to some use and managed to produce such a detailed and accurate map, that Mr. Scollick, much to his confusion I expect, was highly commended by the colonel.

As he passed me a ten franc note, the delighted Scollick repeated the Colonel's words of praise and assured me that only one other map had been anywhere near as good, and that had been done by a lieutenant from another company, who was in civil life an architect and surveyor. This was praise indeed.

Early in the New Year we left the village retreat which had harboured us over Christmas, and after various meanderings the details of which I have forgotten, we were swallowed up again by the old familiar Arras with its deep cellars and caves, and its deserted houses.

The town was a place of great military strength and importance, being honeycombed with underground quarry workings, extensive semi-natural caves, and ancient cellars. By piercing the dividing walls, cellar had been connected with cellar and with the tortuous rambling caves, until the whole district had become transformed into a subterranean city the extent of which no individual seemed to know; lighted by electricity and affording accommodation for forty-thousand men. A city beneath a city.

I once spent a couple of days with my company in one of the spacious caves, damp and glittering with dripping stalactites hanging from the roof.

This particular cave had innumerable corridors and passages, some proceeding on and on for miles apparently, others ending abruptly after a few yards as if the excavator had changed his mind and stopped working.

In places, the cave widened out into vast halls columned with glittering piers of limestone which had been left to support the roof, and along the main gallery ran a narrow-gauge railway, reputed to serve some underground munition depot.

The enemy, if they wished, could have pounded the city to dust above our heads, but an army could still have lived in security down below.

It was never necessary, however, to live permanently underground, as the town, though pounded daily, was still habitable.

About the beginning of March our officers' mess was located in a smaller and more modern house than the old massive boulangerie we previously occupied, in a dull and featureless street near a public garden. It was a plain street of ordinary middle-class houses, built in rows, with the front doors opening straight off the sidewalk.

One or two houses had been struck by shells, and consequently suffered damage to roofs and upper stories, but on the whole the street remained fairly well preserved, though entirely deserted of course by its normal inhabitants.

The officers dined and lounged in the small salon downstairs with its window abutting the street, using the scrappy furniture left behind by the hastily evacuated owner of the place. A tiled passage led from the front door, iron grilled as usual, to a sort of kitchen at the back where Bert cooked, and smoked, and swore, and scratched himself over the pans, and where we all lounged around between duties.

There were also the remains of a glass conservatory, with a few dried-up plants still left in a few cracked pots, which opened on to a tiny courtyard; a backyard it would be termed in England, and surrounded by a twelve-foot high brick wall.

The domestic quarters were on such a miniature scale, 'cosy and compact' I think the house agents call it, that when Bert stood at the circular French stove turning a sausage or stirring a stew, he would spit right out through the conservatory and hit the brick wall of the courtyard. A trick he was very fond of doing, aiming straight between the plant-pots and out through the broken panes of the conservatory.

At night when the kitchen was shuttered up, and we all gathered round the table playing pontoon or banker by the light of a flaming bit of wick dipped in fat, the place looked quite home-like.

When we had a free moment, Arnold and I and occasionally Blackall, pursued our usual spare-time occupation of investigating the neighbouring houses; scrounging for the common good.

One day Blackall and I entered a house with a broken roof on the opposite side of the street, going in more out of idle curiosity than with any idea of finding anything. As it happened the place had been ransacked before so we found nothing of value, except for another little amusing pottery figure; but looking out of an upstairs bedroom window we discovered a magnificent view of the whole Arras front, stretching right up to the rising ground of Vimy Ridge, then held by the Germans. Destined to be in a few weeks' time, the site of our greatest victory and the grave of many of us.

As Blackall and I hung out of the bedroom window gazing at the limpid blue sky flecked with clouds, we amused ourselves by watching the squadrons of aeroplanes maneuvering high over the lines, and by watching the little white puffs of smoke burst into life all around them, seeming to follow the planes yet always bursting too late to catch them.

It was a sunny March day and ideal weather for the sausage-shaped observation balloons which were also up in full force, like a lot of bloated rubber ducks floating on strings from a pedlar's tray.

While we watched, a squadron of German planes flying very high seemed to swoop down on the sausage balloons, but they couldn't seem to manage it. It was all very clear and bright, the little planes darting about amongst the miniature puffs of cotton-wool smoke, were somehow exhilarating, particularly as there seemed to be many more of our planes, which made it look as if we were winning.

After a while we grew tired of watching for some plane to be brought down in flames, and we took our departure, carrying away nothing but the little pottery figure with which to amuse the vulgar minds of Bert and Arnold.

One evening after dark, when the shutters had been closed over the windows and we were all sat around the tiny kitchen on boxes or on the floor, Bert was busy cooking something for the officers' late dinner, by the light of a solitary candle stuck on the table with its own wax. The dinner, for some reason or other, was timed to be later than usual, about 9 o'clock I believe; when Arnold, snuffing his cigarette and placing the butt-end behind his ear for a future occasion, broached a subject that had been on his mind for a day or two. Namely, the cellar next door.

The capacity of the French for appraising wine and laying in a good cellar is astonishing to the average Englishman, brought up to regard wine as a luxury or a Christmas treat. Middle-class houses such as these would in England, harbour nothing more choice than a half-dozen bottles of Worthington and a couple of gingers, whereas here, a wine-bin fit for Hanover Square was the rule.

"What about it" said Bert, " 'ave a crack at it… if you think there's anything there… but I can't 'elp you, I've got to see this ruddy dinner don't burn."

"That's alright, Bert, there's enough of us without you; but keep yer ear open for Tubby, or Maudie, or any o' them, coming back while we're on the job."

So Arnold and young Bill Dewer scaled the twelve-foot wall of the courtyard, walked along the top in the pitch darkness and dropped down into the next yard.

We heard a splintering of wood as they forced the cellar door, and then silence for some time. Called by a subdued whistle from over the wall, we climbed up and peeped over, to see Bill with a bottle in his hand whispering hoarsely for us to throw over some sand bags to put the bottles in, and to form a chain along the wall to pass the swag over.

'Arnold was in the cellar' he said, 'sampling the goods to see which was the most palatable to carry away'.

Arnold would do that!

We clambered along the wall-top several times, passing down on our side the bottles they handed up, and then we stopped for a few minutes to knock the tops off one or two and 'wet our luck', as Blackall called it. Bert, too, with his eye on the cooking pots, had to wet his luck, and the other two over the wall were wetting theirs we knew.

The upshot was that we all got rather lit up and rowdy, climbing the wall and slinging the sandbags of bottles over with a great deal of hilarity, but still retaining enough common sense to do it quietly.

Every time Arnold returned to the cellar for more bottles he took another drink, and every time he appeared on the wall he was a little more drunk. The drunker he got the further along the wall he wanted to carry the bottles, until in the end he was so drunk that he could not walk without lurching and staggering.

The curious thing was that even in his advanced state of inebriety he could still walk along the narrow top of the twelve-foot wall, in the dark, and carrying a sack of bottles in each hand. I suppose the sack in each hand must have served to steady him like a tight-rope walker's pole, but we were mortally afraid he would fall and break his neck any minute. There is undoubtedly a guardian angel who looks after fools and drunks.

Eventually, as the time was drawing near when the officers would be likely to return for their late dinner, we got Arnold to desist from repeating his tight-rope performance, and persuaded him to lie down in an unobtrusive corner and sleep it off.

"Shove all the bottles out o' sight somewhere" advised Bert, "Charnst the gendarmes come nosin' rahnd."

So we carted them up to the attic and hid them behind a pile of rubbish where a shell had once knocked a hole in the roof. About a dozen or so we kept behind in the kitchen and when the officers returned, Blackall carried in their usual mess of potage, and then, with a poker face, very grandly served the wine.

"Where d' you get those from" snapped out "Tubby" Edwards, as soon as he laid eyes on the bottles.

"Just found 'em lying about loose, sir" said Blackall very innocently, "among a lot of old rubbish, sir. We've got a few more in the kitchen, sir."

"Well, you've no business to find anything loose" began Tubby, when Maude and Backlake chimed in "Oh! Come on now, Tubby, you old Puritan, drink up and ask no questions" pouring out another glass, "C'est la guerre, you know."

"C'est la guerre be damned, I don't like it," persisted the punctilious Tubby, "This is conniving at loot and accepting a bribe, and they've no business to do it."

Free drinks are hard to resist, so Tubby's conscience was finally outnumbered and jollied into an unwilling acquiescence, his scruples drowned in the careless jollity which rapidly became the keynote of the evening.

After Blackall's return to the kitchen with the news that they were 'mopping it up alright', fresh bottles were broached and a very convivial evening ensued, though as it takes a very little wine to put me under the table, my recollections are somewhat blurred.

The sequel to our escapade arrived the next day, in the shape of a crabbed, querulous-looking Frenchman pushing a hand-cart. We watched furtively as he parked the cart against the kerb and, unlocking the door with a key, entered the house we had raided.

"That must be the bloke himself come to fetch 'is booze away," remarked Blackall to me as we listened attentively for the 'bloke's' reaction to an empty cellar.

"Well," I said, "we've got rid of all the empties, so he'll have a job to trace it to us."

"Shurrup!" cried Blackall, with his ear to the wall, "he's found it."

And at that moment a terrific commotion, a banging and a shouting in French, broke out next door, sounding like a dog-fight in the cellar. The noise seemed to flow out into the street, so we rushed to our front door, opened it cautiously and looked out just in time to see a most comical sight.

Clambering out of the cellar window was a Scotsman, his foot apparently being gripped by the irate Frenchman in the cellar, who was yelling 'blue murder'. Freeing his foot with a vicious kick, Jock scrambled out of the cellar-window and went haring up the street for all he was worth, his kilts flying as he ran, before the Frenchman could scramble out.

The flying Scotsman's unmistakable kilt absolutely cleared us of any implication, and we watched with much amusement as the frustrated Frenchman shook his fist after the fast disappearing Scotsman, cursing "Les Ecossais", and yelling "Brigand! Voleur! Sale vache!"

So Scotland's reputation for nosing out free liquor remained supreme and unimpaired; fortunately for us.

All was not over however, for on the following day a couple of very determined looking gendarmes walked in our front door, demanding from the captain, permission to search the house. They got it of course and then commenced to rummage in every nook and cranny.

All over the kitchen they poked and pried, in the cupboards, behind the stove, examined the red tiles of the floor, then to the upper stories they went while we listened apprehensively to their tapping of the floorboards.

Arnold remarked in an aside while the search was going on, "Cheer up, boys! They can't do more than shoot us, and the Jerries will damn soon do that."

We saw with relief that they returned empty-handed from the attic; the sum total of their search amounting to nothing more incriminating than a few bits of broken bottle from the yard, which they examined for marks of identity and smelled very suspiciously, but in vain.

So they departed, after solemnly warning the officers that they were certain we had had most of the wine but couldn't prove it.

13

The day after the incident of the flying Scotsman I 'clicked for fatigue duty'. In other words, was caught by a sergeant and impressed into a working-party bound for the front line.

Those working-parties were the bane of my life and I always tried to keep out of the way when I knew one was being made up, as every other sensible dodger did. Being a company runner enabled me, if no legitimate excuse was on hand, to 'disappear' until the party was safely formed and on the way.

One might think that when the troops were not actually in the firing-line they were away back in Arras, resting and recuperating. Such was not the case, for though they might be out of the trenches they were not resting. In reality they were often trudging up to those very same trenches two or three times a day, or night, working harder and more dangerously than those in permanent occupation of the front line.

Whenever there was a job to be done, and there always was, it naturally fell to the lot of the P.B.I. (Poor Bloody Infantry) who were resting in reserve to do it. Sometimes it would be digging a new trench under cover of darkness, or re-digging and old one that had been blown in by the enemy. Sometimes it would be humping the hundred-and-one varieties of stores up a couple of miles of slimy trench, often in the middle of a dark night, with the stray phone wires catching your burden at intervals and your foot finding the hole in a broken duck-board.

Heavy rolls of barbed wire, massive baulks of timber, bags of concrete, bundles of iron corkscrew posts for upholding the wire, sacks of trench-mortar bombs, as well as daily rations, all had to be carried up by that same old pack-mule, the infantry in reserve. And how they did curse and swear on those trips! Blinding, blasting and bloody-ing at the frequent aggravations and exasperations!

There was a popular rhyme which ran:

God made the bees,
The bees make the honey,
The infantry do the work,
And the R.E.s* get the money.

* R.E. Royal Engineers, and a reference to the fact that they were paid a little more that the Infantry Regiments.

A division of labour and reward which I have noticed is customary in many walks of life.

The party I was constrained to join consisted of fifty or sixty men who were led off through the town in a single file, headed by Lieut. Backlake, who alone knew the nature of the job to be done.

The file wended its way like a schoolgirls' crocodile, along a street of tottering walls, around a huge pile of stony rubbish which not so long before had been the beautiful 16th century Hotel de Ville, and so into the Petite Place.

Of the two adjacent squares, Grande Place and Petite Place, the Little Square had suffered most. On the side facing the German shelling nearly all the gabled house-fronts had fallen outwards into the square, leaving a tangle of hanging floors and gaping rooms exposed to the next pulverising shell. On the opposite and safer side of the square, the picturesque arcading of the shops still remained to give a little shelter from flying shrapnel. The centre of the square where once the busy market-stalls had stood, was now all holes and rubbish and distinctly unhealthy for idle loitering.

As we passed under the arcading the shriek and crash of a shell rent the air and another house on the far side of the square shuddered down in a cloud of dust.

As we turned the corner a dead man lay sprawled on a heap of stones, his limbs bent back at unnatural angles, like a discarded rag doll stuffed with sawdust.

Onward in phlegmatic silence moved the party, through ancient narrow streets, out into the newer open boulevards by the railway line, onward still further to where, alongside a smashed factory wall, started the trench named "Iron Street"; so called I suppose, after the masses of rusty broken machinery which littered the vicinity.

A hole in the ground almost lost behind a heap of broken bricks turned out to be the entrance to an old cellar, and at its sandbagged mouth the file of men came to halt, each man in turn disappearing down the opening for a moment and emerging with a heavy burden on his shoulder.

"Toffee-apples" growled those at the head of the queue with disgust. "Perishing toffee apples."

Toffee apples… The word passed along from mouth to mouth like an evil rumour, acquiring with each repetition a more lurid adjective and the objects themselves a more obscene destination.

'Toffee-apple' was the soubriquet applied to a species of trench-mortar bomb. It consisted of a huge iron ball as big, or even bigger, than a football, filled with explosive and attached to the end of a three-foot steel bar as thick as your wrist.

The bar was thrust into the muzzle of a special trench-gun, which when fired sent both ball and handle sailing over into Jerry's lines, there to explode with a terrific crump. They were frightfully destructive, blowing yards of trench into the air at one bang. A toffee-apple fit to blunt the teeth of Mars himself.

As my turn came I descended the six or seven steps into the cellar, and endeavoured to pick up the toffee-apple indicated to me by the bored sergeant-in-charge. It was a terrific weight. I could not get it up on to my shoulder at first, until the next man in the queue gave me a hoist up with it. Once there, I had all my work cut out to stagger up the steps with it, and, with crambling knees, join the tail-end of the straggling line of men just entering Iron Street.

After proceeding along about half a mile of winding trench, we halted a moment to get our breath and rest the toffee apples against the side. I dare not put mine down, knowing that I was not strong enough to pick it up again if I did.

One red-headed Welshman, Ginger Lewis, being too fed up with the thing to care what happened, plumped his down in a patch of sticky mud, exclaiming "To hell with it!"

When word was passed along to 'pick up again', the smooth ball was found to be held so tightly by suction that it could not be shifted; not even by the combined strength of all who could gather round to grasp the handle. So, much to the secret delight of Ginger Lewis, it had to be abandoned.

After a long, and to me, exhausting trip, the front line was reached at last and the toffee-apples dumped at the appointed place. On being freed from the irksome burden we departed swiftly, and with a feeling on my part as of a camel that had lost its hump, but mighty pleased and relieved to be on the way back with the job done.

The pleasure and relief were somewhat premature however, for on emerging from "Iron Street" into the rubble-strewn road, the file was halted once more before the cellar opening.

"What are we 'anging abaht 'ere for?" grumbled those in the rear who couldn't see any reason for the stop.

"For Christ's sake git on with it in front there."

But as the real meaning of this halt slowly dawned on the men it was realised that yet another trip had to be made, a swelling ripple of gaudy and picturesque blasphemy ran down the ranks. At such moments the art of swearing rises to heights of inventive obscenity undreamed of by 'nice' people.

Backlake, strolling along the queue, commiserated with the men and assured them that one more trip would finish the job, and that this time the burden was not to be the detested toffee apples, but sacks of Stokes bombs instead. Not quite so bad perhaps, but bad enough.

That part of the German front which was scheduled to get it in the neck soon after we had delivered the consignment of Stokes bombs, zig-zagged along about a quarter of a mile beyond the local cemetery.

To reach the line with our load, we followed a trench which ran for some distance under the lee of a railway embankment, then turned suddenly aside to cut clean through the cemetery ground itself. Over the top of the trench could be seen, blown all awry by the frequent bombardments, hundreds of those tastelessly elaborate monuments which the French erect over their dead.

Stone crosses with curly iron fittings, rusty tin wreaths, glass globes of celluloid flowers with a faded photograph of the deceased nestling amongst the celluloid petals and bleached almost white with long exposure to the brilliance of successive summers.

The glass globes were all shattered, the headstones all drunken and chipped; the very coffins themselves, disinterred and split open by high explosive, lay about with their bony tenants exposed to the light of day.

One or two of the old family vaults had been enlarged and deepened and fitted with wire netting beds, so that the living Thomas Atkins might sleep more peacefully than the dead citizens of Arras.

Not that these converted vaults were popular as sleeping quarters; far from it. Many wouldn't sleep there at all if the other dugouts were full, preferring to lie down in the open trench rather than slumber fitfully with the ghosts in that old tomb.

As the man in front of me remarked while we were passing through these cemetery trenches with the bombs and discussing the question, "It must make yer feel like John Brown's body sleepin' in them tombs, sort o' mouldering in the grave. We'll be ghosts ourselves soon enough without 'ob nobbing with 'em."

Then, changing his grip on the sack of bombs dangling over his shoulder and increasing his pace, he added, "Roll on when we get out o' here. All these blasted bones lying about gimme the willys."

Eventually we arrived in the front line with our load, were met there by a dashing young lieutenant of the trench-mortar battery, who strangely enough seemed keen on his dangerous job, and told us to dump our sacks in the funk-holes.

The Stokes bomb was a type of trench missile fired from a gun of very simple but very effective design. The gun itself consisted of little more than a short metal tube with a spike at the bottom, which detonated them; then out they came again with a rush and a swish, describing a high arc in the air and landing in Jerry's lines with a crashing explosion. Stones and dirt, sand bags, baulks of timber and sometimes human bodies soared into the air at every crash.

When dropping a shell down the barrel, it was advisable to pull your hand back smartly and to suppress any instinctive inclination you might have to look down the spout, otherwise your head and hand would be likely to accompany the shell over into Jerry's lines as it rebounded out.

It was possible for an expert gunner to drop the shells down the muzzle so quickly that a steady stream of four or five could be maintained in the air at once, which must have created over at the receiving end a devastating and nerve-shattering effect.

Trench-mortar men were extremely unpopular with the soldier in the line. And no wonder, for wherever they went, destruction and death stalked at their heels as an inseparable shadow. It was their grim business to pay flying visits to certain chosen spots in the front line, giving their crashing Guy Fawkes display and then, as rapidly as possible, move out of harm's way again.

Their arrival in itself was a death sentence; their passing-by, a longed-for reprieve.

Fixing their mortars in the trench they would study the enemy trenches through field glasses for a while, fiddle about for a few minutes getting the exact range and then, at a pre-arranged signal, throw over in a few short minutes all the hundreds of shells we had laboriously carried up for them; blowing the German trenches to bits, and thus provoking Jerry to furious and instant retaliation.

But it was not the business of the trench-mortar men to wait for the retaliation. No! As soon as their spectacular show was over, their shells all expended, they faded silently away in prudent haste; away from the hornet's nest they had aroused, but leaving the unfortunate company holding the line to grit their teeth and swear, as the retaliatory bombardment broke around them

As mere carriers of the unpopular load, our duty that afternoon was done with the delivery of the bombs. So away we went down the communication trench before the storm broke, followed by the envious eyes of those unfortunates who had to stay behind and see it through.

Just as we had got as far as the cemetery on the way back home, the racket started. The quiet stillness of the late afternoon, which up to then had been broken only at intervals by the occasional whine and crack of a solitary sniper's bullet, was violently disturbed by the rapid rattle of bursting Stokes bombs.

Ginger Lewis, who happened to be the next man following hard on my heels as we trotted home down the trench, cast an appraising eye backwards towards the racket, gave a long drawn-out whistle in imitation of a shell arriving and remarked facetiously, "They're off! As the monkey said when it fingered the circular saw; so Gawd 'elp the sailors on a night like this."

In a few moments the whole front was ablaze, aroused from its somnolence like a sleeping monster suddenly poked in the eye, and the artillery on both sides began pounding away at each other.

As we trudged grimly along the narrow trench, shells started dropping in the cemetery around us, throwing up columns of dirt and breaking up still further much fractured gravestones.

Pandemonium reigned for a time, but we trudged unhurriedly on. Unlike those poor devils up in front we were homeward bound.

Then, as suddenly as it began, everything quietened down again. The rattle and crash faded away into a spasmodic crackle of distant rifle fire and gradually the peaceful stillness of the spring-like afternoon was once more restored. The only alien sound to remain being the homely clump! clump! of our heavy boots on the duck-boards and the sharp 'patter' of cockney witticisms.

The "stunt" was over.

Villers au Bois
Mont St Eloy
La Targette
The Labyrinth
La Folie Fm
Neuville St Vaast
Les Tilleuls
Thelus
Farbus
Arleux
Fresnoy
Willerval
Bailleul
Oppy
Ecurie
Roclincourt
Gavrelle
Marœuil
Anzin
Ste Catherine
St Nicolas
Le Point du Jour
St Laurent
Athies
Fampoux
Rœux
Duisans
ARRAS
Dainville
Blangy
Feuchy
Tilloy les Mofflaines
Achicourt
Warlus
Monchy
Beaurains
Agny
Wailly
Guémappe
Neuville
Wancourt
Vis
Rivière
Ficheux
Héninel
Mercatel
St Martin
Hénin

Book 3

14

Returning to the town just as the dark shadows of evening were beginning to gather, I dragged my leaden feet along the dull street back to the billet; fed up, dog-tired, plastered with mud and exhausted with the carrying of loads too heavy for my strength.

The working party on its return had been refreshed with dixies of steaming tea, extra special tawny brew for hard working men, but by the time I turned into the billet and clattered down the tiled passage into the kitchen, I was ready to accept the chipped cup that Bert thrust at me with the words "'ave a drop o' char before these greedy swine scoff the lot."

On the principle of "never say no" I accepted the proffered cup of "char" highly sweetened and thickened with a liberal dose of condensed milk, and sank down wearily in a corner, thankful for the chance to relax at last. After sipping the over-sweetened tea for some moments, I felt better and more disposed to listen to their half-chaffing questions as to "what's doing up the line? - 'ave you bin chivying the ruddy Jerries again?"

My replies only confirmed the opinion that a new 'push' was in course of preparation and started a heated argument as to when and where the storm would break; whereupon Blackall, suddenly turning to me, remarked inconsequently, "Come and 'ave yer photo took with me tomorrow, will you, Clayton? I have found a place this afternoon where they do it cheap. Six postcards for five francs. You come in with me young 'un and we'll 'ave three apiece for f.2.50."

"Fancies 'isself with 'is 'ansome mug" put in Bert with some truth, for Blackall was always inclined to be a bit dandy and at that very moment was busy polishing his already bright tunic buttons.

"Three postcards'll never be enough to go rahnd that harem o' yours you left in the Walworth Road" he added with a grin.

"Never you mind my harem," retorted Blackall, breathing hard on a button, "it would be three postcards too many if your ugly kisser was on 'em."

"Well!" interposed Arnold, trying to turn the argument to his own advantage, "I always say 'ansome is as 'ansome does. Got any more char in the pot, Bert?"

"Yus, but we aint got no more milk" replied Bert, holding the empty milk-tin upside down.

"Darky, there," pointing at Blackall, " 'as scoffed the lot."

"Never mind. Give us the tin!" and Arnold, bending back the half-opened top with his jack-knife, poured some hot tea straight into the tin, swished it round and round a few times to wash the milky interior and drank up.

I agreed to share the six postcards with Blackall, so on the following day when the mud on my boots and puttees had had time to dry and been scraped off, we set out to find the photographer Blackall had discovered.

In a narrow side street just off the Rue de Gambetta we found him. A short, little, elderly Frenchman, too old and stout for active service, his protuberant corporation had pressed against so many tables, had bulged out his waistcoat to catch so many soup drippings that the cloth shone with the hard service, plus the ample lubrication.

One wondered why he chose to stay behind in such an unsafe place as Arras. It hardly seemed possible that the few miserable francs he made out of the troops could be sufficient compensation for the lack of safety and civilised comforts.

Photography can be such a useful art in the right hands - and the word "spy" flitted unbidden through my mind, but I banished the uncharitable thought.

Dressed in a shop-walker's seedy frock-coat worn over his ordinary shabby suit, he welcomed us with a quick little bow, polite but business-like. He motioned us forward with a fat little hand outstretched, into the bare dusty studio, lit uncertainly from above by means of a cracked skylight.

Against one wall a crinkled backcloth hung like an old roller-blind. In front of this stood one of those rickety bamboo tables generally found supporting the family aspidistra in small cottage parlours.

Instead of the peace-time aspidistra however, there reposed in burnished glory on a purple velvet cloth one large shell-case and two nose caps, while on the shelf underneath, a larger and heavier "dud" shell completed the collection and served to steady the table.

"Avec les souvenirs, Messieurs?" queried the little man, indicating the collection as he placed Blackall in the chair and stood me behind.

"Wee, wee, avec souvenirs tray bon" replied Blackall in what he fancied was fluent French.

Blackall, the finicky dresser, had taken care to 'posh himself up' before we came. Brushed his tunic, polished his buttons and badges, and wound on his puttees carefully in even spirals.

We had left our tin hats at home as not being smart enough for the occasion, and as we waited there set stiffly in the photographer's conventional pose while he dived under the black cloth and focused the camera, Blackall carefully tilted his forage cap to the right doggish angle. That studied, rakehelly angle so assiduously cultivated by all young cockneys out ogling the girls in the High Street, interviewing a book maker, or on some other sophisticated errand.

"Le képi M'sieur." The photographer withdrew his head from under the cloth and indicated with expressive hands that I too should tilt my hat to the same rakish angle.

"Ze 'at sir. A leetle more élan. Comme ça," tilting his head to convey the meaning. And as I did so, "Ah! ça va bien M'sieur, ça va bien."

With everything set he held up an admonishing finger and rapped out, "attention pleese!"

Silence, while we gazed unblinkingly at the lens.

Click!

With a quick little professional bow and a resounding "voila, messieurs! C'est fini" the little man indicated that the business was over.

"Demain matin à dix heures, mais maintenant cinc francs s'il vous plaît M'sieurs" holding out his podgy hand and rubbing finger and thumb together as if counting notes.

"What he say?" demanded Blackall.

"They'll be ready tomorrow at ten, but he wants the dough now" I explained.

"Oh! The hell 'e does," bridling a little at the idea of paying in advance, "Don't trust us far, do 'e?"

The little man sensed a difficulty and explained that we might be killed by a shell in the night or leave suddenly for the trenches and never return, in which case his work would be wasted.

"Well, for that matter a shell might fall on his shop in the night, then we'd lose both photos and five francs as well. Ten francs in all" argued Blackall.

We paid up however, and promised to call for the six postcards on the morrow. Which we did, and found them all ready for us.

I sent my three postcards straight home and as I write they lie before me, but whether Blackall ever lived to see any of his three again, or whether he died in one of the many adventures which later befell the Battalion, I shall probably never know.

Handwritten on reverse: "Clayton and Blackall 1917"

Not very long after our visit to the photographer, the week before Easter to be exact, we moved into a dungeon-like vault which rampled around and beneath the foundations of several old shops near Petite Place; the most ancient quarter of the town.

It was window-less, cold, clammy, and the massive stone piers which merged imperceptibly into the arched roof, half-filled the place with their rough-hewn bulk. The vault itself was extensive yet shapeless. A meandering tunnel between the piers, passing from dim recess to dim recess.

The air was vitiated by a crowd of waiting men, their scattered equipment and sprawling legs tripping the careless walker at every turn. They lounged, smoked, spat, played cards, or just told bawdy stories to pass the tedious hours; while the steady flame from many candle-ends and fatty dips cast an uncertain light over khaki coats and stacked rifles.

Down here underground we could feel as well as hear the rumble of the bombardment which had been steadily growing in volume over the past three weeks, and the hour was fast approaching, we knew, when it would burst into a sudden crescendo.

Bert and Blackall, Bill Dewer and Collimore, Arnold and I, and the rest, sat idly on our packs on the stone floor. There was little else for us to do. It was a period of waiting.

Collimore, as was his nature, endeavoured to be cheerful and chatty.

"Did y'ear about that bloke from "D" Company" he remarked.

"No! What did 'e do?" queried Blackall.

"He went 'ome to Blighty on seven days leave and never come back for a month."

"Did they find 'im and fetch 'im back then?"

"No! 'E come back 'imself this morning and they shoved 'im straight in the clink. They've run 'im for desertion, so I expect he'll be court marshalled."

"What did 'e do it for then, the silly b------r, if 'e was going to give 'isself up?"

"Well, he told the Sergeant-major," continued Collimore, "that if he'd got to be bloody well shot, he was going to have a bloody 'oliday first."

"I don't blame 'im neither," commented Bert. "If it'd been me I wouldn't 'ave come back at all till they fetched me."

Towards the evening of Easter Sunday a flicker of interest travelled around the crowded cavern. The rumour passed from mouth to mouth arousing the men from their ennui: "Over in the morning --- Over the top in the morning - pass it on --- Over the top in the morning. - s'right. Straight from the 'orses mouth."

"Roll on, then," commented Arnold as the rumour floated by. "If its got to be, let's get it over, quick."

Then in humorous vein as he caught sight of Bert's ugly impassive mug, " 'Ave yer made yer will yet, Bert?"

A quizzical glitter animated Bert's fish-like gaze for a moment as he replied in a similar vein, "Yus, I done it. 'Alf in trust 'til the kids is twenty-one, 'alf to the old 'Trouble and strife' for 'er lifetime, then all to the kids when she pegs 'aht."

Flicking the ash off his sleeve in pseudo-grand manner, "We gotta think a bit afore we croaks, y'know, we landowners."

"You don't say, Bert!" put in Collimore, "I never told you, did I, that I used to be a landowner once."

"No! You never!"

"S'a fact. Free 'old too; but somebody shoved it orf the window-sill."

"Garn!"

And so, in spite of many a quip and jest to relieve the tedium, the hours dragged on.

We were expecting to leave the vault at any moment to go up into the front line, so no one attempted even the partial undressing which was the common preliminary to a full night's rest; but just lay nodding in corners, rifle close at hand and equipment ready to slip on in a jiffy.

It would have been a tremendous relief to me to have taken off my puttees, if only to have had a good scratch at the chats which I felt sure were walking up and down my legs, but the business of winding them on again would have taken too long had the call suddenly come.

About one o'clock in the morning things began to move. Captain Tite, Scollick and one or two other officers appeared in the vault, the N.C.O.s began bustling about, and a lashing of rum came round.

The gloomy outlook brightened considerably with the advent of the rum and before long a rowdy sing-song was under way. Whether it was a spontaneous reaction due to the rum, or whether it was purposely organised to keep the troops occupied during the last hour of waiting, I couldn't rightly say. Probably the latter, for I noticed that whenever a halt in the singing seemed imminent, either one or other of the officers, or the

Sergeant-major, would keep the ball rolling by suggesting a fresh song.

The spirit of this sing-song however, was something quite different from the usual drunken, care-free bawling which went on in estaminets. This was the last desperate roaring of condemned souls endeavouring to keep their courage up, and grimly determined to squeeze as much pleasure as possible into their one remaining hour of life.

As 'pleasure' to the untutored mind, and to many a tutored one for that matter, is often synonymous with dirt, it naturally followed that the nature of the songs became increasingly depraved.

Starting off with the harmless drinking song, "I'm Major General Worthington, Worthington, Worthington," the programme rapidly deteriorated into a series of unprintable parodies of popular airs, dirt being capped by more dirt, until in the end sheer vulgar obscenity held the stage.

In the ordinary way this would never have been tolerated by the officers, but it was obvious they were rather shamefacedly letting the poor devils have their fling. Their last carouse.

To such straws of pleasure does human nature cling when faced by eternity.

At last, as the songs touched the lowest depths of bawdry, the order came to move. A sudden scramble to don webbing equipment and sling on the gas-mask satchel, a hasty grab at the rifle, a quick glance round to see that nothing had been forgotten, and we left the gloomy vaults for ever, without even troubling to snuff the guttering candles.

Forming up in the street outside in that chill darkness which precedes the dawn, I felt an overpowering sense as of one more desperate venture launched beyond recall. The stakes were on the table. The cards were cut. Nothing now could arrest the inexorable process of destiny.

It remained only for the croupier, Death, to turn the card and claim the stakes, or forego his claim once more.

As the platoons assembled in the narrow street and moved off one by one, the dark night sky was suddenly shot with a film of grey. It was the dawn; and so quickly did it spread that by the time we had traversed the short streets debouching on to the Rue de Douai adjoining the railway line, it was day.

'The' day! Easter Monday!

Crossing the rusty metals and threading our way through the rubbish of a flattened suburb, we were soon standing in the front line, awaiting once again the 'zero hour".

Zero! Nothing! Nil! The point from which all reckoning begins, thought I, recalling my old school textbooks and the droning voices of the masters who expounded them.

Whether it is possible for events which are still enveloped in the golden mists of the future to oppress or cheer, or in any way affect the spirit here and now, has never to my satisfaction been proved. Apprehension or foreboding in the face of an obvious danger is an understandable thing. Prescience, or any pre-view of the future at a time when all seems calm and changeless, appears to me, on the other hand, to be a far more doubtful quantity.

Whether or not then, this thing called prescience has any real existence or is merely another human conceit - whatever the reason the fact remains that once we were assembled in the trench, all the gloom of the past few hours fell away and gave place to a cheerful optimism. Something, I couldn't say what, rose-tinted the picture for us. Success was in the air.

Our barrage was heavy; the German barrage light; and the trench was crammed with well-tried comrades. All seemed in our favour. What more could one want?

Or perhaps it was that I was merely getting accustomed to that cold jump off into eternity and didn't give a damn what happened.

15

The Battle of Arras which opened in a snowstorm on Easter Monday 1917, was in its first stages one of the most notable successes of the war.

Ever since the early days of 1914 the German heel had been firmly planted on the outskirts of Arras. German guns day by day had pounded and splintered her ancient stones. And German eyes had scanned the town and directed the firing from the high ground of Vimy Ridge, four miles to the north-east.

The attack aimed to capture this valuable ridge and at the same time push back the invader to a more comfortable distance from the town. In this we were more than successful, for the 1st and 3rd Armies under Generals Allenby and Horne operating on a twelve mile front, pushed back the enemy in the first two days to a distance of five miles and seized the formidable ridge.

At one stroke Arras was freed from the enemy's grasp and the Ridge was ours for keeps.

The plan of attack was well conceived and had been assiduously practiced before the event, so everyone knew exactly what to do when the big moment arrived. Three weeks of increasing bombardment by our artillery culminated on the eventful morning in a crashing roar, which was followed up by line after line of infantry, moving forward in wave formation behind a creeping barrage of bursting shells.

The idea was, for the first wave to advance a certain distance and then lie down, for a second wave to pass through them and do the same, and for the third wave to follow suit, pressing on still further.

Numerous lumbering tanks assisted the infantry, a sky-full of droning aircraft hovered low over the advancing front reporting progress, and a corps of engineers and labourers followed close behind, fixing phone wires, levelling roads and laying sections of light railway-line as fast as the ground was captured.

In addition to the railway and the meandering River Scarpe, several main roads radiated from Arras in the direction of the neighbouring towns of Lens, Lille, Douai and Cambrai.

The one of these roads which I came to know best, the Cambrai Road, was a typical Flanders highway. Straight as a ruler, slightly raised above the surrounding fields, its avenue of trees casting cooling shadows across the curving camber of the stone sets, it diminished down a long, straight perspective towards its distant vanishing point in the direction of Cambrai. In the triangular sector formed by this road and the railway to Douai, over its sea of shell-holes, lay our particular job of work.

As we first jumped out on top on that Easter morning, the wind blew cold and fresh and a few flakes of snow swirled this way and that.

I kept my eyes glued on the line of bursting shells just in front and watched as it swept forward in short, precise jumps. It is a good rule to keep close up to your own barrage on such occasions; to lag behind may mean that you get caught amongst the exploding shells of the enemy's counter-barrage.

The German front line soon yawned at our feet amongst the smoking pot-holes. It had been immobilised here for so long that it had attained a moss-grown old age; but the occupants of the ill-fated place were either repulsively dead, or gone.

On we pressed over the pock-marked ground, stumbling up and down the smaller holes, round and about the bigger ones, almost lost in an undulating sea of hollows and ridges. Several other hoary old trenches materialised amongst the holes, showing evidence of the years of patient labour expended in their digging, their timber shoring, their sandbag revetting, but now all scattered wide.

Though I saw in the distance one or two shell-bursts cause gaps amongst the advancing groups of men, no one near me seemed to be touched. These distant tragedies I observed out of the corner of my eye, with the cold impersonal detachment with which one views the funeral of a total stranger; and the anguish of the mourners. The drama might be happening on the moon.

We trudged steadily on and on in extended order without catching sight of a single live German and were finally told to lie down in a shallow depression, a one-time draining ditch, which came athwart our path.

"All dahn in the ditch - pass it on - all dahn in the ditch!"

"Which ditch, Sergeant?"

" 'ahndsditch, yer silly coot! All dahn in the ditch, there!"

We half lay, half crouched in the depression in perfect order, everybody seeming to be present and in high spirits, as if this were merely one of those mock battles we had practiced so often and in which no casualties ever occurred.

Then I peeped over the edge of the ditch and saw that it was no mock battle.

Up a sloping ridge of ground, I saw innumerable grey-green figures, backs bent, heads down, running for all they were worth. First one then another of the fleeing figures would appear to stop dead in his tracks and be left behind to form a still, grey blob on the brown earth.

Perhaps about half of them reached the top of the ridge and disappeared from view over the edge of the skyline.

The stuttering rattle of one of our machine-guns away on my right explained the uncanny failure of the rest to reach the skyline.

I heard close behind me the boyish voice of Lieut. Maude - a little overwrought and excited, I thought - and turned round to see him sitting on the rear edge of the shallow ditch. Beside him sat a boy of about his own age, but dressed in the same grey-green uniform as the fleeing figures I had just observed.

Maude was trying, in a few halting phrases of schoolboy German, to question the youth as to the whereabouts of his comrades.

"Wo sind dien kamerad?" he kept on repeating.

"Wieviel kamerad haben sie?"

But the youth seemed either not to understand, or to be too dazed to reply. He gazed straight ahead with unseeing eyes, like a young rabbit accidentally caught amidst a pack of hounds, dumbly but patiently awaiting the end.

I looked curiously at the peculiar cut and colour of his tunic, examining its strange shape and the over-amplitude of its fit, and then I stopped and gaped with astonishment. My disbelieving eyes had encountered a round hole in the very centre of the ill-fitting garment, a tiny trickle of red actually oozing out as I looked.

He had been shot right through the body, in a place I should have said meant rapid and painful death, yet strangely enough, he seemed totally unaware of it.

"He's been shot, Sir" I said, pointing out the hole in the middle of his tunic.

"By jove, so he has!" exclaimed Maude, seeing it for the first time. "We'd better send the poor blighter down to the dressing-station, then."

But whether his wound suddenly proved fatal and he dropped dead on the way, or whether he reached the dressing-station and outlived the war in some prison camp, I have no means of knowing.

It was the last time even that I was to see Maude, for just at that instant we were ordered to get up out of the ditch and continue the advance.

On and on we went, up and down the hollows, until the muscles of my thighs ached with the continual rise and dip, rise and dip of the shell-torn earth.

From our slightly elevated position I caught glimpses of the more remote sectors of the battle line stretching away to the north. The silver gleaming ribbon of the River Scarpe turned and twisted its way along a slight valley, while beyond its further bank away in the extreme distance I could see the rising slopes of Vimy Ridge dotted with tiny, bursting puffs of smoke.

Though occasionally obscured by driving mists of sleet, the distance was not so great but what I was able to distinguish: the flying kilts of some Scottish regiment as they raced up the steep slope. The 'women from hell' as the Germans called them.

"Go it the Jocks! Give 'em ginger!" roared someone as we plodded on, much in the same voice as he would have bawled "Come on Arsenal!"

The way seemed to be getting harder, the holes bigger, until finally the ragged line of men became broken and divided by the sheer size and number of the holes to be negotiated; split up into parties of five or six or even into solitary individuals wandering alone.

After a time, finding myself thus isolated and alone, I decided to sit down in a large shell-hole which offered its sheltering cavity just at that moment, and give myself a short breathing space to review the situation. It needed only the concussion of bursting shells just in front of me, however, and the hum of flying splinters, to convince me that I had come far enough.

I had rested there for only a few minutes, wondering what the next happening was likely to be, when a khaki form - I was glad to see it was khaki - scrambled over the lip of the hole and flopped down beside me. Pushing back his tin-hat, the form wiped a perspiring brow on his coat sleeve; a sleeve ornament, I observed, with the braid and single 'pip' of a Second-lieutenant.

A lean familiar face looked into mine and seemed pleased to see it was me. It was Scollick.

At first I hadn't recognised him in the 'Tommy's' uniform which all wise officers now wore when going over the top; to prevent them from being picked off by discriminating enemy marksmen.

He seemed to be labouring under some excitement and his first words on regaining his breath revealed the cause.

"Just have a look at this, Clayton!" pointing to the collar of his tunic. "I seem to have got it in the neck by the feel of things. Can you see anything?"

"You have, sir, but not exactly the neck I replied, examining his shoulder. "You've got a lovely 'Blighty one' there. A bullet clean through the top of your shoulder just below the collar bone."

"Does it come out at the back?" turning for me to see.

"Yes Sir, clean as a whistle. It must have just missed the top of your lung. Can you feel anything?"

"No, not much." And visions of England, Home and Beauty showed in the pleased grin which spread over his not unhandsome features as he realised his luck. I looked at him with envy and wished a slice of luck like that would come my way too.

Much might happen before his vision was realised, however, as was at that moment demonstrated.

A swish, followed by a terrific crash only a few yards away, hurled a humming shower of iron fragments over our heads and we both instinctively ducked.

"Seems a bit of a hot spot just here," he observed; "That was one of ours if I am not mistaken. We must be right up to our own barrage unless the careless blighters are dropping 'em short. Look here, p'rhaps you'd better take a chit back to the Batt. Headquarters and tell 'em to get the barrage lifted. Tell 'em they're dropping the blasted stuff on us."

"Right, sir!" I replied, though privately thinking that it was our fault for advancing too far.

His arm was not too stiff to prevent him writing, so he scribbled the chit on a leaf of his field-notebook, signed it and handed it to me.

"Do you think you'll be alright here, Sir, with that shoulder," I asked, as I pocketed the chit.

"Yes, I'll be alright, but you keep out of the way of that gun, Clayton," he warned, as I scrambled over the rim of the hole. "Cheerio! Good luck!"

The gun to which his warning referred was a German machine-gun which still remained unquelled in the area we had just captured. It could only be a matter of time before its isolated gunners were 'mopped up' with half a dozen well placed Mills bombs, but just at the moment its staccato fire continued to rake round and round in all directions wherever a khaki tunic showed above the broken ground.

Bobbing up and down the shell-holes I made a wide detour to avoid attracting its fire and after a good deal of searching, managed to find the battalion dugout and deliver Scollick's chit.

Brisk and busy in his dugout with a couple of signallers tap-tapping their Morse beside him, "Dolly" Cooper paid scant attention to the chit. It was old news by that time, anyway.

"Very well, Orderly. No answer!" he snapped out, and turned immediately to other business as I gave him the usual waggling salute, turned on my heel and departed. I felt disgusted at having come all that way with a useless message.

Plodding back once more to the advance position and keeping a sharp look out for that gun, I suddenly stumbled into the short remnant of a German trench, and into tragedy.

A small group of three or four men were gathered there around a recumbent figure lying on a sort of fire-step at the side of the trench. A moaning and crying came from the figure and as I looked over their shoulders, I found myself gazing into the chalky-white face of young Bill Dewer.

He was half-conscious, moaning and babbling incoherently and crying bitterly.

A large piece of shell had passed through his left arm just below the shoulder, severing it, except for a little retaining skin on each side.

Nothing could be done.

While his life ebbed into the soil, they were trying with roughly sympathetic words to soothe his ravings until the stretcher-bearers arrived.

"Take it easy, kid, we'll soon 'ave yer 'aht of it now!!

"You' got a 'Blighty' this time, boy, and no mistake."

"Take it easy, kid! Take it easy!"

He seemed to be dying.

I turned away with a heavy heart and, resuming my journey, found on my return that the tide of battle had flowed onwards far in advance of the place where I had left it. Fresh troops had pressed in with the advance, leaving my Battalion well in the rear, to 'mop up' and generally consolidate themselves into an effective reserve line.

My company had collected in an old German reserve trench, blown flat in parts, and were just beginning to gather themselves together again into a coherent unit. Every few minutes fresh arrivals would wander along with the question, "Anybody seen the Sussex mob?"

"Yus, mate Further on."

"Seen any o' the West Kents abaht 'ere?"

"No, we aint."

"Anybody seen the Buffs?"

" 'anging on the wire at Loos, mate."

"Fusiliers?"

"Yus, pal, 'ere y'are. Fusiliers this way."

Though the time even yet was barely mid-day, I was dog tired and wearied almost to a standstill with the rough going, which had been continuous from the time of our first jump off at dawn.

Now for a little breathing space, I thought, leaning my rifle with its fixed bayonet against the side of the trench and seating myself on an earthy bank. I had been carrying the thing about with me since dawn and never fired a shot out of it the whole time.

Shells and machine-guns. When these two have done their work little remains for us to do but walk over and occupy the ruins. And as for personal protection, I would much rather have had a good revolver that this heavy rifle, made longer and more unwieldy still by the tin-opener stuck on the end of it.

Barely had I relaxed my weary limbs on the earth bank than they were galvanised into action once again by the urgent call passed along from mouth to mouth.

"Orderly! Orderly! Orderly wanted this way!"

And along I had to go, though inwardly fuming. Where the hell has Arnold got to? I thought. Am I the only blasted orderly in this company?

It turned out to be the Captain who wanted me.

"Go back to Batt. Headquarters and show the Colonel the way up here" I was commanded!

"Hell and damnation!" I swore to myself. Back over that same wilderness of shell-holes again, when already I could scarcely lift my feet off the ground for weariness. Surely he must be able to find his way as well as I could.

In due course I arrived once again at the Battalion dugout and presented myself to the Colonel. No sooner had I done so than he greeted me with a cold, impersonal "Come along, Orderly." turned briskly and set off on the return journey, while I following hard at his heels, made my fifth crossing that morning of the detestable wilderness.

As fresh and lively as some jungle-cat he danced over the shell-holes with his usual hopping gait, and at such a pace that I could hardly keep up with him. The blighter seemed made of spring-steel.

It may be fit and proper that the directing brain of the battalion should not be burdened by mere equipment, but as he pranced on in front of me, I envied him his freedom to stand up lithe and active under nothing more weighty than a service revolver and a light cane.

I was supposed to act as his guide and bodyguard, but in my present state of exhaustion the boot would be on the other leg if we did chance to meet any prowling Boches.

Fortunately we didn't, so that ticklish problem never arose.

16

Dolly Cooper bounded on his way again after inspecting our positions, and without requiring me to accompany him further, I was very relieved to find. I felt just about 'all in' by that time and glad of the long overdue respite.

Bert stuck his bayonet into the side of the trench and hung his mess-tin on the handle in vain endeavour to make a drop of tea, but the whittled splinters of wood which he used were too damp to burn.

Arnold, and later on Blackall, appeared at last over the hillocks of earth and scrambled down into the trench, full of their adventures and gasping for a 'drag' at the one solitary Woodbine they were able to raise between them. It turned out that they had been helping to silence that isolated machine-gun, which had continued to pump out a spray of lead from its concreted emplacement long after the main body had been thrust back.

They had pitched bombs at it for an hour or so and then rushed it with the bayonet.

They also brought news that young Maude had 'gone west', killed by a bullet in the stomach. It must have happened during the second part of our advance and very soon after I had seen him interrogating the young German.

Another one gone. How many more before it all finishes, I wondered?

I thought of the fear and trepidation with which he had set out on this his first 'over-the-top' experience; of his distrust of his own courage and of his dread that he might involuntarily quail before the terror of the critical moment; of his fatherly platoon who carried him safely over that dread moment on the wave of their simulated sang-froid; and of the famous name he bore without after all disgracing it, as he feared he might.

Innumerable shells continued to swish overhead, but as most of the German light field-guns were in our hands, it was mostly a one-way traffic in our favour. Nevertheless a few roaring rushes high up in the sky, as of aerial expresses travelling the other way, denoted that enemy heavy stuff was on its way to Arras.

During the afternoon the company was moved over to a wide-open, desolate sweep of ground, abounding in holes and muddy ruts but in little else. Not a glimpse, not a vestige of any kind of shelter from the elements broke the monotonous disorder of the battlefield.

To add to the discomfort, a cold penetrating wind drove gusts of sleety snow across the gloomy landscape, and the black drizzle slanting down, united muddy sky with muddy earth. The very acme of desolation reigned supreme as far as the eye could reach.

There was nothing to eat but a tin or two of salt bully-beef. Hacked open with a jack-knife, the tin's gristly contents had to be laid, bit by bit, on to a thick army biscuit and held there with grubby forefinger until consumed; or else speared with the jack-knife point and conveyed directly to the mouth. It was unpalatable tack that only a starving man would eat.

" 'Orse flesh. That's what it is, mate. 'Orse flesh."

The biscuits themselves were of the dog variety, square and hard as an earthenware tile. 'Iron rations' they were called and iron rations they felt like. No wonder they don't take men with false teeth into the army.

The leaden sky grew muddier still, darkened and faded into premature night, leaving us with the problem of where to lie down and sleep. Somewhere between sky and earth I supposed, as we couldn't stand up all night like horses. Sublime wretchedness supervened. Abject misery prevailed.

"Hoy!" called Bert to Arnold who had been nosing around a good deal, "fahnd anywhere to kip, yet?"

"No . It looks as if we shall 'ave to dig our own kip tonight."

"What abaht that place over there?" asked Blackall, pointing to a straight-cut furrow a few yards away.

"Is it a trench?"

"No. Somebody's started one, but its only about a foot deep. Still it'll 'ave to do for me." replied Arnold. "There's no other place."

So, along with the others I went over to it, laid down on my waterproof sheet in the furrow, wrapped my great-coat around me, and rested my head in the hollow of my tin-hat to keep my face off the wet ground. Neither the drizzling sleet, the shrewd wind, nor the uncomfortable posture, prevented me from sleeping the instant my face settled into the tin-hat. It rained, it snowed and shells lobbed over, but I slept on until daybreak.

When I eventually awoke, stiff and cramped, and with a dent in my face from the tin-hat, a pool of slushy water half-filled my portion of the furrow, oozing and squelching as I lay there in it, soaked to the skin on the underside and encrusted with snow on the top side.

"Christ! What a kip!" commented Blackall with chattering teeth. "What a blasted kip! Shall I tell you what I could just do with, this very minute?"

"Wot?"

"A nice cup o' corffee," smacking his lips at the vision, "Scalding 'ot - and filled up to the brim," he added slowly, "with a nice drop o' fe-fi-fo-fum."

"Don't make me larf, I split me lip." replied Bert, beating the air with his arms to restore the circulation.

"The nearest you'll get to it mate, this side of Arras, 'll be a whiff o' the Sar'ut-Major's bref."

With the passing of the night the weather took a turn for the better, the Sergeant-Major and one or two officers appeared - I don't know where they had slept - and we were moved up nearer to the front, though still remaining far enough away from the enemy to allow us freedom of movement without the necessity for cowering in trenches.

We were thus idling about in the vicinity of an old communication trench, cleaning our rifles, scraping the dirt off our tunics and puttees, watching the planes maneuvering and darting about, or just reducing the 'chat' population in the seams of our shirts, when a sudden warning shout came from somewhere:

"Get in the trench, quick! Dahn in the trench, you mugs! In the trench quick!" Then, "Look aht, 'ere they come!"

And as we tumbled in, hot foot, a Fokker 'plane zoomed down out of the sky with a roar and flattened out within a few feet of the ground, its machine-gun stuttering away at full blast all the time. As the machine skimmed the top of the trench the two sinister black crosses painted underneath the wings loomed disquietingly near and large, and the goggled face of the pilot became clearly visible as he leaned out of his cock-pit to view the damage.

The said damage being, miraculously, nil; for all had managed to roll, jump, or throw themselves into the trench in time; and some, quick on the trigger, had managed to take a pot shot at the intrepid pilot with their rifle.

Luckily he had no bombs to drop on us, but it was an abject lesson on the wisdom of keeping large parties of men within diving distance of a sheltering trench, despite the fact that our own 'planes commanded the air.

As well as trenches there were several ex-German dugouts we could have used for shelter, deep and strongly timbered, but until they had been properly examined and all booby-traps removed we were not permitted to use them.

Jerry had a habit of leaving a spade, or perhaps a pickaxe, lying carelessly across the lower steps for the unsuspecting 'Tommy' to kick aside as he entered in search of souvenirs. Or maybe a fine spiked helmet would be resting on the rough dugout table, left apparently in all innocence by some hasty Oberleutnant. The fact that these articles were connected by concealed wires with a charge of high explosive would not be obvious in the dim light, until both dugout and souvenir hunter sailed up to heaven in one blinding flash.

We were not again required to make contact with the Germans - somebody else was doing that - but were kept in reserve for four or five days more, living amongst the holes and debris of the devastated battlefield.

During my wanderings about the area on orderly duty I came across some strange sights. There was the time when I passed along a well-beaten track on my way to the Battalion dugout, and returning the same way a few minutes later, found that a shell of truly enormous proportions had buried its steely nose in the footpath. Walking gingerly round it, that shell appeared to me to be about the size of an average dustbin. It was a 'dud' of course, but I did not tap it to see how dud.

Then, on another trip, I encountered a curious object; an object that had been flung bodily high into the air by some searing, singeing force, and had fallen back to earth in a form which put me in mind of a tattered brown bolster from somebody's old settee. It was just as spineless and featureless as that. Sort of shapeless all over.

I gazed at it for a moment and then passed on with a shudder, saying to myself, "so that's what happens when a shell explodes at your feet."

In another place, our rapid advance had so got the Germans on the run that a troop of cavalry had actually been able to gallop into action.

"By gad, sir, that's the style!" I can hear the white-whiskered old brigadiers roar from their club chairs.

"Get 'em on the run, Majah, what! And let the cavalry show their mettle. Show 'em what horse-flesh can do, sir, and to hell with their tanks!

Go into action like a gentleman, sir, with a spirited mount between your knees, what! Not like a damned plumber hiding in the belly of a 'Tin Lizzie'."

But the dashing troop of cavalry could only have been at the start of their run, could indeed hardly have started at all, when the fox turned round and bit 'em; caught them and stopped them with a salvo of shells just as they breasted the rise and came into view of his battery of guns.

The belly of a horse is less resistant to shot and shell than that of a 'Tin Lizzlie', so there they lay in shocking heaps, where the whirring iron of bursting shells scythed through them. Lacerated lumps of red meat; stinking offal for some spewing 'conchie' to clear away.

In the fighting line the hours move for the combatants with an incredible slowness. A day seems like a week, a week like a lifetime. And every lingering hour is supercharged with possibilities, holds within its sixty minutes the capacity for startling change. One moment is filled with horror, the next with alarm; one with misery and exhaustion, many with sheer boredom; some moments even with humour, joy, or elation.

Of these joyful moments probably the most pleasurable is that glorious one when the relieving troops arrive. When some other 'mob' comes up the line to take over and we gladly pass on to them the legacy of privation and danger which it is now their turn to endure; ours to relinquish for a while.

At last that happy moment arrived for us, and our earth-caked feet were soon striking the pave' - what was left of it - down that straight perspective of the Cambrai Road, back to Arras. The road, its sides littered with smashed waggons and dead horses, was shell-scarred and long. But in its very length a tribute to the magnitude of our recent victory.

Arras itself was different. Freer, busier, livelier. The overhanging, menacing shadow of the double-eagle had been banished. One no longer need remember to walk to the left side of the Rue de Douai because the right side was a speedway for spent machine-gun bullets.

The ancient Petite Place, once a place perilous to cross, had now recovered some of its rightful atmosphere, that of a busy market-square. The vehicles which came and went were still not farmers' gigs, however, but gun-limbers and ammunition waggons; and the standing traffic not market stalls, but pot-bellied Company cookers belching columns of acrid smoke from crazy tin chimneys as the cooks boiled up the stew.

Under the shelter of a ruined shop-front just off the Petite Place, a loud-voiced, jovial, but extremely wary individual was running a crown and anchor board.

"Bookie" was written all over his hard-boiled face despite the khaki tunic. With one weather eye open for the approach of an officer - gambling was forbidden - he plied his trade.

In a voice now bawling and blustering, now cajoling and persuasive, he induced the small crowd of patrons to part with their franc pieces, their five and ten franc notes; to cast the shining silver and the greasy paper on to his dirty square of cloth, on the off chance of trebling their stakes as he uncupped the dice.

The cloth was divided into six compartments, each embroidered with a diamond or a spade, a heart or a club, a crown or an anchor; and on to whichever of these seductive sirens pleased you most, you laid your money

"Where you liked and where you fancied," as the operator described it.

"Who says a bit of the old mud 'ook, the lucky old mud 'ook?" he bellowed, referring to the anchor.

"Roll up and lay your money where it can't lose" he went on, with just the suspicion of a wink. "Cast your bread upon the waters and see it come back with jam on it. Put your trust in the British Navy, boys, and back the lucky old mud 'ook. Britannia rules the waves boys, 'an always will."

Then having got enough money laid on the anchor, the luck apparently shifted over to the ace of spades, for he changed his tune and bawled, "How abaht the old ace o' diggers? What! Nobody says a bit on the lucky old trenching iron?"

"Come on, Darky," he continued, singling out Blackall who was standing with me in the crowd at the time, " 'ow abaht a flutter on the old digger. Back your own division, mate," - the ace of spades was our divisional sign - "it can't lose."

But Blackall was broke and I didn't gamble, so there was no response from our direction. Finally, seeing that no more bets were forthcoming, he rattled the dice in its wooden cup, gave a quick glance round for any last-minute punters and sang out, "Any more for anymore, any more for anymore? No? Then up she comes an 'er colour's blue!" Emptying the dice-cup with an elaborate flourish.

Necks craned forward hopefully. Expectant eyes watched the two dice as they rolled onto the table, wobbled uncertainly, and then settled with the anchor and the heart uppermost.

"What did I tell yer," roared the Bookie, as if he'd known all the time, "The lucky old mud 'ook's done it again! The 'eart and the mud 'ook wins agen," omitting to mention the unlucky spade he had tipped so certainly to win.

As he scooped up the loser's cash and paid out the winners, we turned away and passed along the street in the direction of our billet. The meaningless, oft repeated patter commenced afresh, floating after us faintly on the breeze; "Roll up, roll up and chance yer arm! You come 'ere in rags and go away in motor cars."

"Some o' them blokes is rollin' in dough," observed Blackall, as we traversed the narrow street past the splinter-pitted wall of some church.

"You know I once seen a bloke at Étaples - an Australian 'e was - put sixty eight pahnd on at one go."

"Sixty-eight! That's a funny amount to put on."

"Well it was 'is winnings and 'e left it on the board for the next throw. See?"

"Did it come off?"

"Yus, it did, and I'm telling you no fairy tale. It kem off. And the bloke paid 'im aht at three to one. Three to one, mind, and never turned an 'air, 'e didn't. Never batted an eye lid I tell you some o' them blokes is rollin' in the stuff."

"They must be" I replied, knowing full well that a gamble of that magnitude was quite possible, especially amongst those inveterate gamblers, the Australians.

17

The room I occupied in our latest billet - an upstairs room - had no floor. At least the hole in the middle of the floor was so extensive that only about three or four feet of flooring remained around the walls. Likewise it had no windows, only fragmentary window frames, and no more than half a ceiling.

As I lay on the sound portion of the floor wrapped in a brown blanket with my great-coat laid over as well for extra warmth, I could see straight out between the broken rafters and watch the stars twinkle kindly in the night sky, like silver spangles on a velvet cloak.

Some sort of rash had appeared under my arm pits and around my waist and it itched abominably in the stillness of the night. I wondered if it was shingles. But of course I had doffed my clothes at such infrequent intervals of late that it must be only dirt and the irritation of the ever-active chats.

That particular billet impressed itself on my memory by the way Bert used to holler up through that vast hole in the floor at about 5.30 in the morning, waking us up with a "Hoy! Are you blokes up there all dead?"

It was memorable also for the arrival of a letter from Bill Dewer, addressed to us all from one of the Base Hospitals. He had not died, then, after all. It seems they had amputated his arm - it was as good as amputated when I last saw it - and he was looking forward to going home in a few days' time.

"Well, he's out of it for keeps, the lucky swine" sighed Blackall, as we passed the letter round.

"Yes, he's finished forming fours for good and all," added Arnold, "and what's more," holding out his clenched fist and shaking it, "they can take my bleeding arm too, and welcome, for a pass to Blighty."

"Bah!" spat Bert, who rarely admitted to any craving for home, "Strong words off a weak stummick."

Then, two or three days later, another communication arrived from the hospital - a semi-official letter to the Officer Commanding A. Company: William Dewer, died of wounds on such and such a date, had wished at the last to be remembered to his comrades of the Officer's Mess.

I noticed a glisten in the impassive eye of Bert, that tough old bird, as he wiped his nose on the torn-off bit of shirt-tail he used for handkerchief, and remarked with, for him, unusual depth of feeling, "Poor bahstard!"

All this time the Battle of Arras had been going on. But after the sudden surprise of the first two days, the Germans, rushing up reinforcements from other parts of the Front had doubled their strength; from thence forward any further advances were being contested foot by foot and progress made only at great cost to life.

The battle had become a dogfight. In the words of post-war historians, "The two hostile armies became locked in a bloody and indecisive struggle astride the river Scarpe, five miles east of Arras."

And one day in late April we moved up once more in the direction of the 'bloody struggle." It was my last farewell to Arras had I but known.

The day was fine and sunny as we trudged in single file alongside the permanent-way of the main railway line to Douai. In addition to our equipment, various sandbags containing provisions and the Mess cooking utensils dangled from our shoulders, thus impeding our progress in a measure by causing a minor irritation.

The two jangling petrol-cans of water which I carried slung over my shoulder on a strap, one in front and one behind, evoked in me periodical imprecations at their weight.

But in spite of all, the prospect was distinctly pleasing and would, in less grim circumstances, have claimed to be, in the trite words of the tourist's handbook, a "glorious view". The steel lines sped before us, curving onward under the lee of the railway cutting on our right hand, and on our left where the ground fell away to the river, displaying a magnificent panorama of the valley of the Scarpe and distant Vimy Ridge.

The river wended its way along the marshy valley, expanding in some places to the width of a lake, dividing in others to encompass an island.

On one of these islands a British 'plane, almost as big as the island, had embedded its nose in the earth and cocked its tail to heaven.

"What of the pilot?" I wondered, for shells fell around it continuously.

We plodded steadily on for a couple of miles until several inviting dugouts appeared, burrowing into the side of the cutting and revealing in themselves a striking likeness to primitive cave-dwellings. One of these we found to our satisfaction was to be our temporary resting place.

It as an ideal burrow, felt safe from the heavy shells which sometimes fell on the railway, and the view from the doorway looking over the valley teemed with dramatic interest. About two miles away across the river, Red Cross vans and ammunition lorries could be seen at any hour of the day racing along a much-shelled road, thus providing us with many a thrill as we followed their death-dodging progress with the aid of a pair of field glasses. A really first-class German pair they were, that Arnold had filched from a dead Boche.

Our sojourn in that dugout was enlivened every quarter of an hour or so by a stupefying concussion, the draught from which blew out all our candles, obliging us to relight them each time it occurred.

The first time this happened I swallowed half a cup of tea prematurely, Blackall ducked and swore and dropped the officer's boot he was polishing, Bert and the rest of the dugout occupants also swore and ejaculated the usual query, "Blimey! Where did that one go?"

Investigation revealed the presence - it had been forgotten for the moment - of a huge naval gun mounted on a special rail-bogie which had been shunted up the line under cover of darkness and parked just outside our door.

This out-size in guns, reputed to be a sixteen-incher, pocked its muzzle up to the sky at a high angle from under a screen of wire-netting to which bits of torn canvas had been attached. Anti-aircraft camouflage.

Arnold and I found the firing absorbingly interesting to watch, though the blast of it made our ears sing. The enormous shells were lifted up, if I remember rightly, by a sort of crane, but before they slid into the breech, the jocose gunners would chalk on the steely surface some facetious message, such as: "Put this in your pipe and smoke it" or "Love to Little Willie" or "With the Compliments of J. Bull and Co."

With the breech closed, somebody would twiddle a little brass wheel and the huge muzzle would swing slowly upwards in search of its invisible target, probably miles away behind German lines.

A spout of flame from the muzzle! A barking sort of blast! A rush of air and, if you were standing behind the gun, the shell could be seen for an instant as a diminishing black spot which left the muzzle and swiftly lost itself in the dome of the sky.

As the black spot vanished into the blue we would comment, "That's the stuff to give 'em." Or Arnold would say, gazing after it, "There goes another thousand quid."

A continuous dribble of "walking wounded "limped and hobbled past our dugout door. With legs, arms, heads, bound up in blood-soaked wrappings, they staggered by. Sleeves and trousers cut to ribbons in a hasty attempt to dress the wound, dangled around their limbs as they walked.

The wounded man's natural perquisite, a Woodbine, stuck out perkily from amongst swathes of gory head-bandages. And on every unshaven face around each cigarette played a set grin of undiluted pleasure. The seraphic grin of liberation. They were all going "dahn the line" and some to that soldier's paradise, "Blighty".

Their sentence of death had been suddenly commuted to one of unending cigarettes, English beer, hospital blues and possible feminine adulation. They were heroes who had done their bit and were feeling uncommonly pleased that their bit was done.

They told us with a wealth of blood-curdling idiom that fierce fighting was in progress around the chemical works at Roeux, and that the village of Guemappe was "copping it hot".

An extremely unpleasant prospect seemed in store for us, for we were bound to be sent up there sooner or later.

It turned out to be sooner, of course, and off we went one afternoon just in time to arrive up there at dusk.

Climbing away from the railway, the beaten path led us over the old trench systems of "Brown Line" and "Green Line" - so called I believe, because they were painted in those colours on the Headquarters' maps - over a desolate region where neither tree nor grass, bird nor man, nor any living thing existed.

A rolling monotony of grey earth. Stinking earth. Pock marked and littered, when you came to look at it closely, with abandoned rifles, unexploded bombs, perforated helmets, bits of torn and blood-stained khaki, old boots and parts of wrecked limbers. Over this fetid morass a ribbon-like track worn by many feet, unrolled itself into the distance.

Tubby Edwards in an old raincoat plodded along the narrow track with his platoon strung out behind in single file. I followed in his wake, sticking close to his heels in my capacity as Company-runner.

A screaming swish broke the grey monotony and a spout of earth shot up in front of us.

Tubby stopped, turned, and halted the platoon.

"Move off the path to your left" he commanded, "and lie down!"

We did as he bade and watched, crouching in the muddy holes as a neat row of four shells burst exactly across our path about two hundred yards ahead.

Four more spouts of earth straddled the path a little further along, bursting almost simultaneously.

Then another four further along still.

"Methodical swine, aint they?" observed Collimore at my elbow as we lay on the ground together.

"Its lucky they started before we reached the spot, isn't it?" I replied. "They've got that path nicely taped."

"Right on the bull's eyeball every time. But they must be doing it by the map," he added, "for they can't see what they're shooting at. 'A damn smart bit o' gunnery', I call that."

"They've stopped, thank God!" breathed the platoon Sergeant, as no more spouts disturbed the earth.

"And now let's hope they blinking well give it a rest 'til we get by" he concluded fervently.

The smoke drifted slowly away and vanished, seeming to consume itself.

Tubby stood up, motioned the platoon forward, and the interrupted march was resumed, passing without mishap by the holes we had just seen made and about which still lingered the noxious fumes of burnt explosive.

"Take yer fat 'ead aht o' the light can't yer, and give us a chance to dish the stuff aht,"

In a rough bit of reserve trench situated a quarter of a mile or so behind the ever-shifting front line, half a dozen of us were gathered round the speaker, Bert. Fishing down into the depths of a sandbag he brought up a battered loaf of bread, dirt and hairs clinging to the muddy crust.

Passing the loaf to Collimore - who had recently been doing officers' servant duty - he admonished that individual with the words, "Nah mind, that's not yourn" That belongs to the Mess. And see you 'ands it back agen 'toot sweet' when the show's over!"

"Right you are, Bert," grinned Collimore, "with my dead body I'll protect it."

"You'd better!"

With similar warnings and injunctions the rest of the Officers' Mess victuals were shared out amongst us. To Arnold, some tins of milk and a bag of potatoes; to Blackall, various packages of tea and sugar, jam and margarine, besides another loaf; to newcomers known as "Nobby" and "Shorty", a tin of flour, some coke in a sandbag and an assortment of cooking pots and pans.

Bert himself took some pickles and the remains of a boiled ham; but to me fell the most important item of all, a cold leg of mutton roasted to a nicety.

We were due to go over the top again in a big attack which was scheduled to commence in the early hours of the morning, the third of May, 1917. Hence the temporary share-out of Bert's valuable stores.

I had had an arduous couple of days up here since we arrived in this reserve line. Chasing about from place to place all the time. Up to the front line with a chit, and back again, only to find another chit waiting to go and no runner to take it.

Guides who knew their way about were in constant demand, but guides who did not know had to go just the same.

Only last night I had been sent to guide a full company of men from the next Brigade, along a dreary shell-torn valley I had never seen before, and guide them through the dark night up into the front line.

More by good luck than skill I had managed to locate the correct landmarks in the inky blackness and lead them safely over a nasty bit of No-mans-land, past a derelict tank and into the line without a casualty. Though at one time I thought I had missed that tank in the darkness and their officer, suspecting something of the sort had asked rather anxiously, "did I know the way?"

The Captain of this Company, a stranger to me, congratulated me on their safe arrival and quickly settled his men into position in the trench. No sooner had he done so and dismissed me with the words, "O.K. Orderly! You'd better buzz off back while the going's good," than a gas attack developed.

"That's torn it!" I told myself, as I hurriedly donned my gas-mask and mounted the fire step with the others. "Now I've got to stay with this mob whether I like it or not and see the attack repelled before I dare attempt to cross back again over that No-man's-land."

So I had stayed on, firing into the grey cloud of gas which drifted slowly between the lines, and which appeared to be hampering the Germans rather than assisting them, for none of the attackers got more than half way over to us.

When all was quiet again I had just had time to slip past the tank and over No-man's-land, back to my own Company before daylight.

"Blimey, Clayton!" they greeted me on my reappearance, "You been an 'ell of a time in that shemozzle up the line."

"No, I got stranded up there and couldn't get back, "I had replied.

And now we were preparing for a real big attack. Rumour had it that the affair was to be on a more colossal scale than any as yet attempted. A million men were reputed to be going over on the morrow, but that rumour may have been put about on purpose to give us extra confidence.

I stowed the leg of mutton away at the very bottom of my haversack underneath a spare shirt and some dirty pairs of socks, and on top amongst other personal oddments I deposited two Mills bombs. A couple of cumbersome items that were always handed out to us before an attack, and the carrying of which constituted yet another minor problem. There was no proper place to put the things. The side pockets of the tunic offered the readiest receptacle, but that was marred by the inconvenient bulge which resulted, and by the danger that the safety pin which prevents them from exploding might work out accidentally.

So I usually cursed the bombs and stuffed them in my haversack. An awkward place to keep them, I knew, if I should want them in a hurry.

The haversack packed, I next proceeded to unstrap the steel blade of my entrenching tool from its accustomed place at the side and hang it in front of me like a Scotsman's sporran - thus, a recently discovered dodge to prevent castration by enemy bayonets or flying shell splinters.

Around my neck and hanging like an amulet next to my skin on a dirty piece of string, reposed as always, the red fibre identity disc stamped with my name and number. If I disappeared for ever in a burst of smoke, the disk might turn up again to prove of my demise.

A new cartridge clip in the magazine of my rifle and 'one up the spout' (viz. one round in the breech), and I was ready for whatever might come.

Not knowing the exact time of the attack we sat about in the trench or on the mounds of earth, all ready and waiting.

In the officer's dugout they were finishing off a last bottle of Scotch with the able assistance of the willing tippler, Sergt.-Major Williams, who had been invited in to have a last one. Never-refuse-a drink-Williams.

We waited on.

Daylight faded - darkness crept down and enveloped the scene - and still we waited.

These ante-rooms to the hereafter could grow as boring as any dentist's waiting-room. Almost, it seemed, as if one had to sit patiently until the angel Gabriel in white celestial overalls opened the surgery door and, beckoning firmly, repeated the stereotyped formula: "Private Clayton A., number P.S.10149, you're next. Come this way please!"

18

At last, just before midnight a whisper of something doing flitted along the trench, ruffling the surface of our inactivity like a catspaw of wind on still water. The officer's dugout disgorged its occupants. First the Sergeant-Major bustled along calling loudly for Bates; then the officers themselves appeared, separated diverse ways and proceeded to join their various platoons.

Amongst the men, equipment straps which had been slipped off to ease the wearer's shoulders during the period of waiting, were hastily resumed, rifles clutched and bayonets fixed with a click in readiness to move off.

The curtain was about to go up.

Arnold had been told off to follow the Captain, and I to accompany Tubby and his platoon. Each going to our appointed stations we parted there from one another in the moonlit trench with a perfunctory wave of the hand and "Best of luck".

The last I saw of Bert as he watched us depart our several ways, was that satirical hard boiled grin of his which draped his features in times of stress, and served to conceal from public gaze any glimmerings of emotion he was tempted to feel.

A cloud passed over the moon and his ugly mug disappeared into the black shadow of the trench.

I never saw him again.

I followed Tubby and his platoon into the night, for there was some little distance to go before we arrived at the jumping-off point. A point which turned out to be situated in the open ground of No-man's-land and about thirty or forty yards to the rear of our own front line. When the advance commenced we should have at the outset to leap over that front-line trench before breaking into new ground.

The night was black. Swift-moving clouds had rushed up and covered the face of the moon so that only those individuals nearest to me remained recognisable in the darkness. All the rest of the extended line of men became lost in dim obscurity against the dusky earth; except where the pallid steel of a bayonet exuded its ghostly lustre or the sharp silhouette of a tin-hat cut the nocturnal sky-line.

I knelt with one knee pressed into the loose soil, steadying myself by grasping my rifle held upright like a staff, its stock planted firmly on the earth, its cold, sharp bayonet pointing to heaven.

By my side stood the silent, stocky figure of Tubby Edwards, attired in the same old raincoat and with both hands thrust deep in its capacious pockets.

In the depths of one of those pockets his right hand gripped a loaded revolver while his chin sank in gloomy meditation into the folds of the raincoat's upturned collar.

He was a peaceable, kindly man, pushed willy-nilly by the urgent need of the times into these repulsive, swashbuckling enterprises, so totally at variance with all his natural instincts. Pushed into it, as we all were, by some overpowering force far beyond our control.

Nevertheless Tubby would not flinch at the unhappy prospect, now that it lay before him. He was one of those painstakingly tenacious blokes who would keep grimly on to the very end, patiently doing the job in hand disagreeable though it be, until something cut him short.

I was glad to be going over with Tubby's platoon.

A little further along in the darkness Lieutenant Backlake staggered about amongst his men. This was to be his first time over the top - having on previous occasions been engaged in transport supervision - and quite contrary to his usual habit he had filled himself up with whiskey in readiness for the event. He was consequently fighting drunk and only prevented by the restraining hands of his men from going over before the proper time arrived, to finish off the war all by himself.

The objective of the attack this time, as pointed out by Tubby, was a line of telegraph poles just discernible in the distance away towards the village of Monchy. But to reach it, he warned, there was a considerable depth of ground to be covered as well as two unknown sunken roads to be crossed.

As I peered over the ghoul-haunted mysteries of the enemy territory I could just see the poles sticking up against the sky, but looking no bigger than match sticks, so great was the distance.

Zero hour had been fixed for about two in the morning, "Much too long before daybreak" I thought, considering the distance we had to go. There was a distinct danger, I felt, that we might drift about in the prolonged darkness and lose ourselves on the unfamiliar ground. A misfortune which later occurred.

I would always prefer, if faced by the evil choice, to go over in the dark but to arrive in the light. In effect, to go over at dawn.

At a few minutes to the appointed hour the artillery who had until then given Jerry no inkling of what was in store for them, gradually quickened their tempo.

Stolidly we waited while the guns worked up their demonic overture to a crashing pitch of frenzy… watched while the warning rockets soared up from the German lines in a frantic call for help… and then off we went once more on another hazardous gamble with Fate.

Thrice before this had happened to me. Three times 'over the top' and every time had been different.

The first time a hard-won success had resulted. The second a pitiful fiasco. The third a victorious rout.

What of this? What of the fourth time?

"Now for it!" muttered my nearest neighbour in the dark.

"This is It, my boy! This is the high-jump and over you go! Come along my lucky lads! They're off!"

As the starting tape went up, the drink crazed Backlake, uttering blood curdling yells and waving his revolver round his head like a frenzied devil-dancer, bounded forward into the night far in advance of the rest of us, as if possessed by a fiend. And that was the last time I ever set eyes on him.

As we started to move forward, the more phlegmatic Tubby stepped in front of his platoon and endeavoured to keep them spread out in an extended line by motioning with his hands to those who were inclined to group together, and restraining those impetuous ones who were moving forward too quickly.

The night was far too dark, however, for any kind of formation to be maintained for long, and after the scramble over our own front line all semblance of order was lost. There was, perhaps, no need for regular order as the numbers of men going over were so great that the affair took on more the likeness of a migrating swarm of locusts.

This feeling of a swarm may have been a misconception on my part due to the darkness, but I sustained the impression throughout that I was one of a crowd of shadowy wraiths drifting onwards through the night. One of a huge flight of bats flitting and fluttering, struggling and stumbling along. And amongst those stumbling shadows I saw no face that I knew; heard no voice that I recognised.

I was one of a crowd, yet alone. It seemed as if we were already disembodied spirits fording the final Styx; wandering souls floating between the world of the flesh and the world of the spirit, uncertain yet as to which we belonged. Yet on we sped.

Thus could I imagine the last great trumpet call, when the unnumbered hosts of the dead should burst up through the earth and flock towards the Almighty Throne, knowing not one another.

The crowds of men seemed to float onwards in groups, like wisps of fog blown along by the wind. Yet the drift, strangely enough, did not appear to be all in the same direction. I thought I could see other shadowy groups moving the opposite way but wearing helmets of a strangely squarer profile than usual. And these differing groups seemed instinctively to veer away from each other in the darkness like repellant magnetic particles, reluctant to meet.

Thinking no more of the matter I stumbled onwards, crossing the first sunken road and then the second in the company of several other tin-hatted spectral forms.

I ought to have stopped long ago. I was an utter fool not to have done so. Exactly why I went on I cannot explain. I can only think that I must have been impelled by a kind of involuntary quest for one thing that could be called a finishing post. I was searching for those damned telegraph poles, as the vagrant eel spawned in the Sargasso Sea speeds home to its native pond.

Having found them, I, and the others with me, came to an abrupt halt.

Daylight found me crouching in a shell-hole along-side a fair-haired youth belonging to some Lancashire regiment. There, about thirty yards in front of us were the telegraph poles; but also at the base of the poles, alas, a trench chock-full of Germans.

We hardly dare peep over the rim of our shell-hole for fear of attracting their bullets.

Things had come to a pretty pass.

I looked behind in the direction from which we had come, I looked to the right, I looked to the left, whichever way I turned I could see no hope. A long way behind us the rockets were soaring palely into the spreading dawn; indicating that Jerry had reoccupied his old front line, or somewhere very near it.

We had reached our objective alright, but we were trapped; maybe half a mile, maybe a mile behind the German lines.

Those square-headed shadows drifting the other way were now fully explained.

We were not alone, the Lancashire youth and I. From nearby shell-holes we could hear the others marooned like ourselves, calling to one another, but how many were there we couldn't tell.

The Germans threw a few of their potato-masher bombs amongst us and received in return a few of our pineapples, but without much apparent damage to either side.

The sun crept up the heavens, his warming rays dispersing the chill mists of dawn and giving promise of a glorious day; but no sun could disperse the chill which gripped my heart. I knew in my bones we were doomed.

We fired a few shots over the rim of our hole but not, I must confess, sticking our heads up long enough to take a very careful aim.

Mechanically we fired, chatting the while about scenes far removed from the present. He had told me in the burred accents of my own native Lancashire that he came from Burnley. Joyfully I had claimed Accrington only nine miles away as my birthplace and, delighted with our kinship, we discussed that pleasant land of our birth.

Our bodies continued to fire and duck spasmodically and await the inevitable end but our minds played over the moors and fells of our beloved county; our inner eyes dwelt on those lovely red brick smoke-stacks soaring up in opulent dozens from humming, thriving mills; our ears transmitted the rattle of machine-guns into the glorious clatter of clogs on granite sets.

And then it happened!

Somebody a few shell-holes away bawled to those around, "we gotta get back to our own lines. Let's all rush it together, boys!"

With that, a few bombs were hurled at the German trench and in the ensuing confusion we all rose out of our holes like a flight of crows from a ploughed field and legged it back in the direction from which we had come last night.

Maybe there were twenty of us, perhaps thirty, dodging and ducking in the hail of bullets which immediately followed our rush, flicking up spits of earth around our feet.

In case the reader should at this point suspect us of "living to fight another day" it needs to be pointed out that there are times, as any chess player knows when the only move left on the board is backwards; and the need for that strategic retreat is made doubly urgent when machine-gun bullets are pattering round your feet like summer hail. So we hastened homewards.

I was progressing well, I thought, putting a safe distance of undulant ground between me and the rattling gun, when suddenly… something seemed to hit my left foot with the force of a flying brick… and I rolled head over heels into a shell hole.

The roll probably saved my life, for as well as raking the ground with the machine-gun - I could still hear its stutter - large numbers of Germans were now standing out in the open firing their rifles from the shoulder.

I examined my foot but, to my great surprise, found the blood now staining my puttees had its source at the knee. Another fellow had rolled unhurt into the same hole and he helped me to cut a slit in my trouser leg, break the little phial of iodine on to the wound and bind up my gory-looking knee with a strip of emergency bandage we all carried.

All this time we were both watching closely and apprehensively the movements of numerous German soldiers who now seemed in complete possession of the field and were wandering this way and that firing into the ground. At what, we could easily guess!

And then, whether from the excitement, or from the loss of blood, or from both causes, I don't know; but for the first time in my life I unaccountably fainted.

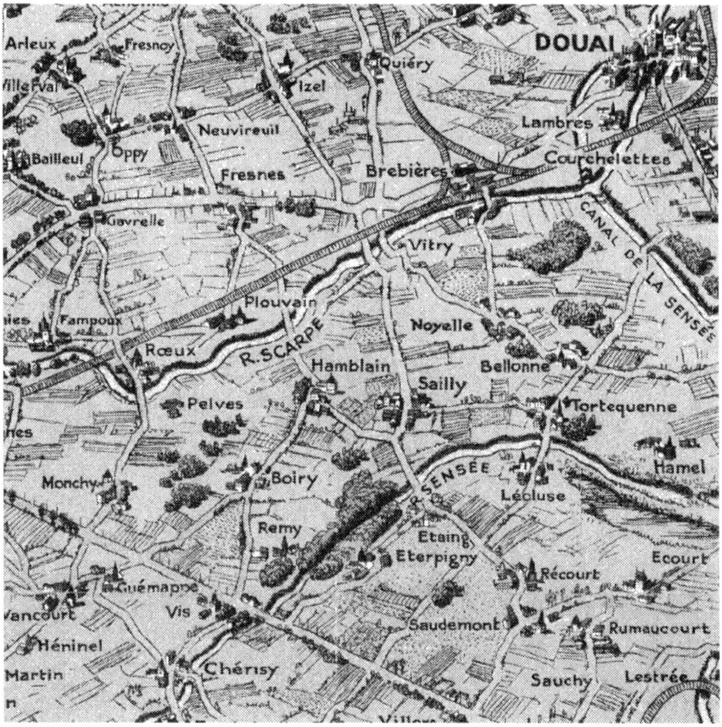
Arleux
Fresnoy
DOUAI
Quiéry
Izel
Lambres
Neuvireuil
Oppy
Bailleul
Courchelettes
Fresnes
Brebières
Gavrelle
CANAL DE LA SENSÉE
Vitry
Plouvain
Fampoux
Noyelle
R. SCARPE
Rœux
Hamblain
Bellonne
Sailly
Pelves
Tortequenne
Hamel
Monchy
Boiry
SENSÉE
Lécluse
Remy
Etaing
Eterpigny
Ecourt
Récourt
Guémappe
Vis
Saudemont
Rumaucourt
Héninel
Martin
Chérisy
Sauchy
Lestrée

Book 4

19

I came to in lonely solitude, with the soft warm rays of a glorious May day sun warming my face. I could see his shining brilliance almost overhead, so the time, I thought, must be about mid-day.

Intense quiet pervaded all. Not a rattle, not a rumble broke the beautiful stillness. The whole world lay basking in a perfect noon-day peace, needing only the waving corn and a warbling lark soaring up into the sun's golden disc, to achieve heaven.

I turned stiffly in my little shell-hole and peeped over its edge.

Five yards away a khaki soldier knelt on the ground with his face turned to the east, his forehead touching the earth in that humble obeisance with which all true believers praise Allah.

His face was hidden from me so I could not tell whether it was my late companion of the shell-hole or not.

Neither could I tell what had killed him in such a curious position, a bullet or a bayonet.

Raising myself on my elbow I looked around and saw, scattered over an area of perhaps half an acre, more khaki figures - quite a company of them - all biting the dust in a variety of curious postures. Some lay flat on their faces, some lay with limbs drawn together in agonized retraction as if resisting a sudden colic, while one or two were arched up precariously on their knees like the nearest one to me, looking as if a slight push would roll them over. There were probably thirty or forty of them, posturing there in rigid fixity; about as many as had attempted the ill-fated dive back.

The whole grisly company lay mutely oblivious of the living noon-day sun. Lay with the soundless immobility of a petrified forest. Not a limb twitched, nor a finger stirred, and I sank back into my hole again with the consciousness that I alone of all the company remained alive; stranded an unknown distance behind the German front.

I resolved forthwith to stay in my hole until dark, and then try to crawl back unobserved, but the problem of how I should cross the German trenches when I came to them, I left for later solution.

The long, golden afternoon drew to a close; the purple dusk rose like a mist from the ground and I prepared to crawl out of my hole as soon as the afterglow had departed from the western sky.

It was only with great difficulty that I did eventually climb out, for every time my left foot came into contact with the ground the bones of my knee seemed to grind together, and red-hot needles shot up and down my leg. I flopped over into the next shell-hole in perspiring agony and rested a moment.

But this will never do, I thought, rousing myself, the night will be gone and I shall be forced to lay up another day; so more slowly still I flopped over to yet another hole and rested again.

I was just gathering my strength for another flop over, when a metallic sound cut the night and smote my startled ears. The sound of a pick and spade clanking together, to be followed later by the dull thud of many feet striking the earth with a shuffling beat.

No need to ask who they were. But would they see me, and what would they do about it if they did?

I crouched low in my hole in the darkness, waiting expectantly with one eye cocked open in the direction of the sound.

Then they appeared. A straggling file of the hated Jerries in their ugly square-headed helmets. Carrying picks and shovels they tramped close by my hiding-place, but happily without seeing me. Obviously a working-party on their way up to the front line.

They had all passed safely by, I thought, when one, carrying a rifle, wandered rather nearer to my hole than the others had done and apparently caught sight of me. He was a nasty, mean looking, oldish sort of customer, wearing that most unmilitary appendage, a beard.

I lay 'doggo', hoping he would take me for a corpse and pass on. But he did not pass. He stopped. I felt his evil stare bore into my back. Heard him mutter a string of guttural sounds which could have been nothing but curses in any language. Then he stooped and picked up my rifle. The rifle I had been dragging along with me from hole to hole and which now reposed on the ground a yard away. He examined it carefully, trying the bolt like some gorilla investigating some strange object. What's he playing with it like that for, I wondered?

The picture I presented must have been ghastly to look upon. My tunic was torn and caked with dirt. My trousers all ripped and smeared with blood, revealed a blood-stained bandage wrapped loosely round a leg shining cadaverously white in the moonlight. I allowed my jaw to hang open as if in death, and put all my trust in the corpse-like effect I hoped to create.

Then the ugly bearded monster raised my own rifle and bayonet in the air. He's going to stick it in me, I thought in a flash. Going to treat himself to the pleasure of sticking at least one Englishman. I could half see the blade, half sense it, poised for the plunge. I waited, not daring to breathe. Just as the pop-eyed frog sits under a leaf transfixed, staking his small life on his protective colouring, so I kept stock still, acting the corpse.

In the space of a split second I expected to feel the penetration of cold steel plunging into my vitals. The crude point probing and lacerating God's perfect handiwork, my human body. But the poised bayonet never descended.

My ghastly tableau served its purpose and the ugly Boche suddenly decided there was no point in sticking a dead body. He flung the rifle and bayonet violently away into the night hurling guttural curses after it, then turned and strode after his vanishing working-party, without even kicking my wretched carcass.

The distance those tramping men seemed to travel and the remoteness of the Very lights I could see soaring up from the front line, began to raise in my mind the suspicion that I could never do it.

Sleep or faintness must have overcome me again, for almost before I was aware of it the night had slipped away and the light of a new day found me in the self-same shell-hole as before with another long wait for darkness confronting me.

The day was again hot though overcast at times, and I passed it in a sort of waking dream, taking an occasional sip of water from my bottle and watching the bulbous white clouds go sailing across the blue. My water was getting low and I began to eye those clouds with interest.

About a quarter of a mile away on a slight eminence, the village of Monchy-le-Preux - I could just see it sticking up - reared its few remaining walls, from which burst forth at intervals the echoing staccato rattle of machine-guns. Monchy, I knew, was a veritable viper's nest of them.

Though I had not been noticing it particularly, an intermittent bombardment had been going on around me. Towards midday this grew to such a pitch of intensity that my failing hopes of rescue were temporarily revived; of a rescue in the only possible way, by another British attack. The more the shells burst around me the higher my spirits rose, until, after one extra near burst, I was disagreeably startled by the searing touch of a red hot-poker on the calf of my sound leg.

A hot splinter of shrapnel - and British shrapnel too - had cut a neat groove through my puttee, and to this day no hair grows on my leg where that splinter notched my calf.

The bombardment, alas! died away again without an attack and my hopes died with it. I was still banking on getting back after dark, not having yet dared to consider any other alternative. After last night's experience no alternative seemed possible.

So when darkness fell at last and I prepared to start crawling again, I immediately received a further shock. My leg, I found, in the cramped space of the shell-hole had set stiff in a half-bent position and I could not climb out. At least, the effort required to drag myself on to the rim was so great that I realised the impossibility of ever traversing the hundreds of holes which must lie between me and salvation, quite apart from snaking unseen across German trenches if I ever reached them.

There seemed nothing left to do but wait for an attack.

That night several working parties passed by again on their way to the front and I cowered down in my hole preparing to act the 'stiff' once more, but they passed without casting a glance in my direction.

Once or twice I caught sight of shadowy figures wearing cross-emblazoned white armlets, rummaging about amongst the shell-holes, and knew them for red-cross men. Whether they were searching for the wounded or searching the dead for rings and watches I didn't know. I wondered whether to show myself to them, for by that time I knew that all hopes of a nice English hospital were practically gone.

It came hard, however, to throw oneself voluntarily into the clutches of that vague, unknown quantity, the enemy, to be dragged off into their grim hinterland and subjected to unguessed barbarities. After all, we had heard nothing good of them for years, nothing but "Hun atrocity" stories, and how were we to know that it was all ballyhoo and propaganda. So I refrained from revealing myself and hung on for another day.

By the dawn of the third day of isolation my blue enamelled water bottle had run dry. The day was dull and chilly, the sun obscured by masses of fat-bellied rain clouds which, however, did not seem inclined to drip for my benefit. With a mouth growing more parched and dusty as the day wore on, I watched those lowering clouds for signs of a blurred edge.

I spread out my waterproof sheet over my legs in such a way that it would catch the rain if any fell, and prepared to drain it off into the enamelled cup I generally used for tea.

The wait was long and my patience went unrewarded until late afternoon, when at last the heavens relented and wept a little onto my waterproof sheet. Carefully I guided the runnels of water as they collected in the folds of the sheet, and drained them into the cup. By skillful guidance I got nearly a cupful of vile, rubbery-tasting water; obnoxious but wet.

In my haversack under the dirty linen, Bert's leg of mutton still reposed untouched and could, if I had wished, have provided me with a tasty meal to accompany the rubbery water. But for some curious reason it never occurred to me to eat.

I wondered how Bert and the Mess had got on without their meat course and reflected wistfully that by now they had probably been relieved and were enjoying the illicit wines of Arras, dubbing me in their bibulous melancholy, "The poor bahstard".

I was getting weaker and knew now the impossibility of ever getting back. Things like gangrene and tetanus had crossed my mind in relation to my wound, so when in the early hours of the fourth day I caught sight of two white-armletted shadows picking their way gingerly in the dark between the shell-holes and the corpses, I decided to hail them.

Casting aside my distaste I gathered strength to make the irretrievable break. Stuck up my arm and croaked out, "Ahoy there!"

As the dreaded enemy approached I saw with relief the red cross on their armlets, pointed to my knee, and repeated the only foreign word I knew describing my condition, the word "Blessé".

They mumbled something remarkably like 'wounded', and started to lift me out of the hole.

Instead of the rolled-up stretchers our men carried, these German "body snatchers" were equipped with the simplest of materials. Nothing more elaborate than a long pole and a big waterproof sheet. Spreading the sheet on the ground they laid me quite gently in the middle of it, gathered up the corners into two loops and thrust the pole through the loops. Then shouldering the pole between them, away they lumbered around the shell-holes, bearing my alien carcass like a roll of carpet, but no less tenderly than they might have borne one of their own.

Eventually we reached a road and the pace increased as my two bearers went dodging and ducking along it in the dark to the sound of many swishes and crashes. It was a new experience to be dodging British shells for a change.

Soon a few ruined houses hove in sight, we stopped before the entrance to a sandbagged shelter at the roadside, I was transferred to its interior, and my two bearers departed up the road again with their pole and sheet.

The shelter was circular inside, extremely low and cave-like, and lit solely by means of an oil lamp-standing on the floor. Its dim light gleamed fitfully on the recumbent bodies of four or five wounded Germans, lying with their feet towards the lamp in the centre, throwing up their grotesque shadows on to the surrounding walls. The place felt cosy and warm; the reek of human odours, of sweaty clothes and drying boots, mingled foully with the smell of the oil lamp. I was the only Englishman present.

The floor light picked out with singularly dramatic accent the features of my neighbour on the left, as he eyed me with quizzical interest. He was a sardonic, Faust-like individual, yet not unfriendly.

Pointing to his bandaged foot and making a noise with his mouth as of a bomb exploding, he explained to me with a tolerant grin, "Englishe granate. Nicht gut!"

I nodded, pointed to my own wound, rolled out a "rat-a-tat-tat" while pretending with one pointing finger to traverse a machine-gun, and enunciate clearly the words: "Mitrailleuse, pas bonne!" I knew no German words for it.

"Ha! Ha! Ha!" he guffawed slyly; then slapping me on the back he winked with knowing pride at its achievement and gave me its name in German.

"Maschienen-gewehr"

The other occupants of the shelter just grunted stupidly.

20

When those two German soldiers had first lifted me on to their waterproof sheet, all the intricate equipment, the tangle of straps, belt, bayonet-scabbard, entrenching tool, water-bottle, haversack and ammunition pouches, with which the government had equipped me to fight its battles, all this had been left behind in the shell-hole. I had gazed back a trifle regretfully at those implements of combat, at those trappings and tokens of my British nationality now sloughed off into the muddy hole, and felt as the butterfly must feel on shedding its unlovely cocoon, released but naked.

In the early morning I was removed from the shelter, dumped on to a proper stretcher and carried further into the ruined village by two dirty, ragged and very crestfallen British 'Tommies' who had been captured unwounded. I saw a few others being herded along in miserable dejection by armed Jerries. It seemed a pathetically unnatural reversal of affairs to see all those lousy Jerries walking freely and confidently along the road as if they owned it, while the boys in British khaki shambled along in abasement.

My stretcher was carried down six or seven steps into a cellar and there deposited on the stone floor by the side of another one, to await, as it turned out, the arrival of an ambulance. The other stretcher also contained an Englishman and as we turned our heads to look at one another the same wondering question rose to our lips, "What d' you think they'll do with us?". In our ignorance we were unable to discover an answer.

Before long the ambulance arrived, our stretchers were carried up the cellar steps, slid on racks in the van, and the closing of the doors imprisoned us in the antiseptic twilight of its interior.

About twelve inches from my face as I lay on the top shelf, two or three jagged holes in the fabric of the van told me more vividly than any words, of its racing, shell-dodging history, and at the same time afforded me glimpses of the terrain through which we were passing.

More quickly than I should have thought we were away from the devastated areas and soon running through the deserted streets of a small town. We bumped over the cobbles at break-neck speed, raced along beside a quiet canal, its low waters reflecting in oily distortion the facades of Dutch-fronted houses, and then stopped with a jerk before what looked like a tin chapel; or it may have been a small school.

The clatter of our approach echoed and re-echoed along the deserted quay, reverberated over the lapping waters of the canal and down the empty streets of shuttered houses, all slumbering in the morgue-like stillness of a Puritanical Sunday morning.

Within the building itself, where we were laid on two adjacent beds, the same prim puritanical quietness prevailed. A calm ascetic female dressed rather like a nun, sat at a desk, the only furniture besides our two beds, in a room of Spartan simplicity. Clean to the point of bareness, the room's only ornaments consisted of a small crucifix, a framed text which I couldn't read, and a ticking clock. We two appeared to be the only patients in the place.

I was getting ravenously hungry. For a full three days I had lain in No-man's-land without eating, so by now it was a good four days since I had eaten anything at all, and more than a week had elapsed since I had last seen a square meal. I looked around and listened but could hear no clinking of crockery, see no crumbs of food, smell no cooking. Did they never eat?

Eventually, one or two elderly soldiers drifted quietly in, were joined by two other nun-like figures, whereupon all proceeded to cross themselves and stand in a group in front of the desk. The prim nun, glancing over them, rose from her seat, made the double sign of the cross on forehead and breast, opened a book and commenced to chant aloud. I could not, of course, understand a word of it.

Now and again the group would join in with a murmured response and then all but the prin nun knelt on the floor, while she recited a long and wordy prayer. None of them took the slightest notice of the two Englishmen lying on the beds only six feet away - we might have been tombstone effigies - but calmly continued to conduct their service in pious solemnity.

It struck me with considerable force, how dead certain they were that God fought on their side.

"Gott mit uns," that to us comic phrase, remained their firm, unshakable conviction.

Ever since entering occupied territory I had noticed the absence of civilians, the clean-swept desertion of the roads, the blank stare of the vacant property, and the strange paucity of war material. Everywhere reigned order, cleanliness, efficiency, but also the most stringent economy.

In comparison with our side of the line where a prodigality of men, munitions and materials, bustled things along upon a wave of lavish expenditure, where the troops if not welcomed, were at least exploited without rancour by cynically good-humoured peasantry - the contrast, I noticed, was startling.

After enduring for several hours the frigid bareness of that pious institution, a fresh ambulance called for us and our journey was resumed, but still no food had appeared.

The ambulance rattled and bumped along at a good round pace, the internal injuries of my partner on the lower shelf causing him to emit a sigh at every swerve, a groan at every pot-hole. In this fashion we must have travelled some miles before finally entering the suburbs of a town, drawing up before the ornate glass and iron of its station entrance.

His case, I supposed, was so serious that they were taking him straight to hospital, for they slid his stretcher out of the van, carried it through the station gates on to the platform, and so out of my range of vision.

I was intensely curious to know the location of the town; so as they lifted my partner out, I twisted my head round and peered through the open door, searching the station buildings for a name. My very restricted field of vision afforded me no more than a narrow peep through the iron gates, and beyond, just a short glimpse along the platform, overhanging which I could see a huge black board. On the board, inscribed in large white block letters, I read "ABORT".

"Now where on earth could that be?" I mused. It must be a fair-sized town to have a station, yet I had never heard of the place. The curious name continued to puzzle me as we turned and drove off towards the town itself, but the real solution only came to me several days later when I saw it repeated in the same giant lettering over another station, in the place where in England we are accustomed to read, "GENTLEMEN".

It was a biggish town as towns go in that part of France, big enough anyway to run a service of trams, and my ambulance ride terminated in the town's busiest quarter with a jolt over the tram-lines, and a swerve-in under a stone archway to the monastic seclusion of an ancient court-yard built within the precincts of some large church.

Within the yard all was bustle and activity. Sharp, abrupt commands were being issued by short-tempered officers in dandified uniforms, and I was promptly conveyed into the body of the church. The interior was vast. Its stony lines soared swiftly upwards in dim and lofty grandeur, its carved and painted roof lost in the mists of its own altitude. Bars of sunlight streamed down through tracery windows, illuminating on the floor below, a scene as strange as any that ancient place could have witnessed.

Between massive stone piers, the whole floor-space was packed tight with British wounded, lying on straw. Packed together so closely, that the over-worked German doctors and the British orderlies, could scarcely find room to step between.

A big, blond Canadian with half an inch of beard jutting out of his face, sidled up, bearing a little tin cup of thin brown liquid.

"Ere y'are, Buddy," he said, handing it to me. "Don't make a beast of yerself."

"What's this?" I asked, sipping the burnt-tasting liquid.

"Well, these b----rs call it 'coffee'," he replied, "But its burnt acorns, and all you'll damn well get from now on."

"What's uh name o' this place, chum?" put in the man next to me, twisting round on his straw.

"Douai. And this is the church of St. Pierre yer in."

"Ow long you bin 'ere?" glancing over the dishabille of the big unshaven Canadian.

"Three weeks, buddy, and the grub's nothing but pig swill," he replied, spitting sideways with distaste at the thought, his eye roving furtively round the church while he pretended not to linger.

"But you'll be all right," he added reassuringly, "They're sending you into Germany."

Just then a sudden burst of martial music filled the church as the great organ crashed into a violent rendering of the "Soldier's Chorus" from "Tannhauser".

We looked up at the organ gallery in surprise and there saw a German soldier throwing his hands about the keyboard with demonic abandon, singing and laughing immoderately as he pulled and pushed at the stops.

"It's that lousy bastard of a Feldwebel agen," growled the big Canadian with suppressed anger, "Sergeant-major to you, sonny" he added as an afterthought, "The dirty rat only does it to annoy the boys, blast 'im!"

A German doctor, sorting out the stretcher cases, picked his way over the crowded straw and indicated me, amongst others, with his pointing pencil. Immediately, I was whisked out of the church, away from the booming organ and the blaspheming Canadian, and loaded with the others on to an open toast-rack tram which had been standing waiting by the church door.

A short ride brought us through a spacious square and so once more to the station, where we were all laid out in rows on the platform, for all the world like a bag of game after a successful shoot.

The hospital train when it slid into the station, far exceeded my expectations. I should not have been surprised to see cattle-trucks and straw. For murderers, after all, cannot expect much consideration from their victims, if the victims happen to escape and turn the tables on their executioners.

But this was luxury. They could have done us no better at home. The beautiful saloon cars were fitted all along the window sides of a central gangway, with white enamelled bunks, upper and lower. Each bunk was a miniature bed, a luxurious nest of clean white sheets; the first I had seen for nearly a year.

They had taken away all my clothes, but my chats were not so easy to get rid of. They clung tenaciously to all the hairy parts of my body, buried their eggs in my pores, crawled under the bandage and dropped onto the fresh white sheets. The irritant malady under my arms also itched abominably. I felt lousy.

So far as I could observe from my bunk, there seemed to be about sixteen bunks to each car with one German attendant who lived on a little seat near the door.

The attendant in my car spoke a little English and so was able to inform us that London was half in ruins, St. Paul's burnt to the ground, and the Houses of Parliament 'Kaput', finished. He seemed surprised at our laughter.

The meals served on that train, though never fattening, were the most eatable I ever tasted in Germany. Never again did I have such a blow-out at the Kaiser's expense.

First came a slice of mahogany-coloured bread. Some hungry optimists gobbled it up in three bites, not realising that it was a day's ration. Then came a watery soup, with bits of macaroni and a few infinitesimal particles of meat floating in it. This was accompanied by one large potato boiled in its jacket; to be followed later by a long, interminable stretch of time, reaching down the vista of the years to the next meal.

The menu varied, of course. Sometimes there would be a kind of semolina pudding with synthetic jam in it. Sometimes a bowl of acorn coffee - if it was acorns; which I doubted. But on the whole they gave us more than we deserved, for they had little enough themselves.

The train rushed on. Stations flashed by my window and were gone. Valenciennes, Mons, Liège. Places famed for lace, for iron, for guns; for historic retreats, for heroic sieges. Then, at Achen, the names turned Teutonic. And at Bonn as we crossed the Rhine, I caught a transient vision of the towers and the turrets, the castles and the crags, of that legendary river.

At Wiesbaden they took out a man who had died. At Frankfurt they stopped to remove some German wounded from the front portion of the train. The crowd on the platform stood sullenly back and glowered inhospitably at the "schwein Englanders". All except an intrepid lady, who rushed forward and swept through the carriage like a benevolent whirlwind, dropping a cigarette on each bed as she passed.

For three days we rolled on by forest and fell, by glebe and glen, past clanking steel-works and plodding peasants, through the smoke of cities and the scent of pines, until we stopped right in the middle of Bavaria, at a town named, "Ingolstadt".

Postscript

'Ingolstadt' remains the last word in Albert's story. We do not know whether he intended to write more. The last chapter ends halfway down a hand-written page, followed by several unwritten sheets; so the evidence suggests he stopped there, and perhaps as this was the end of his active service it was an appropriate place to finish.

Survival as a prisoner of war may have been a very different experience when compared to his journey up to this point. Perhaps this was a story he decided not to tell, or the telling of it too hard. Unless further evidence comes to light, we can only speculate.

A search of Red Cross records confirms Albert as a prisoner at the camp in Ingolstadt. He is detailed in three lists. The first confirms his capture at Arras, dated the 3rd May (presumably the date when most prisoners were taken); entering the Ingolstadt camp on 9th May 1917.

He next appears on a list of prisoners at the military hospital Ingolstadt on the 8th August 1917. Later, he is listed with other POWs moved from Ingolstadt to another camp at Beyreuth, around 100 miles to the north. The document implies they left the Ingolstadt camp on 15th March 1918, arriving at Beyreuth on the 18th March, leaving again on the 4th April 1918. It will take further research to add detail to these final months as a POW before he was repatriated.

We are fortunate that Albert's story was not the last place we read the word 'Ingolstadt'. A rummage through family documents turned up an intriguing group of photos, which we can now make sense of for the first time.

Aside from the three photos of Albert and Blackall taken in Arras, a handful of postcard portraits appear to show soldiers who are most likely fellow POWs. Some cards are inscribed on the back; all printed by a local Ingolstadt photographer. Without further investigation, it will be unknown how these individuals may relate to Albert's last months of the war. Amongst the photos, however, we are fortunate to find a picture of Albert himself (overleaf); slim, in hospital clothing, stick in hand, dated August 1917 - around 3 months after capture

What do we read in our narrator's face - the defiant stare of a captive survivor; the hint of a smile?

After the war Albert returned to study at Leeds and graduated from the Royal College of Art in 1922. Three years later he married a very talented graphic artist, and fellow graduate of the RCA, Elsie Mary Evans. They travelled Europe together painting the architecture and landscapes of Belgium, France, Italy, the Netherlands, as far as Prague. Had the war inspired a desire for travel?

Elsie died from an illness in 1936. She was only 35.

Albert settled in London and became a highly regarded teacher of art in different institutions. He still kept in touch with old and distant friends, and in 1949 married Greta (Lucie Marguerite) Dufty whom he had known since art school – another highly talented artist, poet and writer of short stories. At the Leeds School of Art she had known the sculptor Henry Moore, who wrote to her from the trenches during his own army service.

Albert retired in 1970. I fondly remember him and Greta as an elderly couple who regularly attended our church, Albert dressed in his brown suit and trilby hat.

When they became too old to travel, we would often drive out to visit their home in Wanstead on a Sunday afternoon. I can picture Albert, now frail and bedridden, straining forward to make himself heard and chatting with Dad in an animated way about art, and heaven knows what else.

He died in 1981 at the age of 86.

Albert's war memoir has been a wonderful family discovery, and it may resonate for others who have had family members live through a similar experience. More broadly it may add colour and detail to our collective military and social history. The dry historical facts of war can appear to have little relevance without some connection to our own lives, and we thank Albert for representing his memories of this time in such a personal and immersive story.

No doubt, there will be more to discover.

Micah Duckworth
February 2020

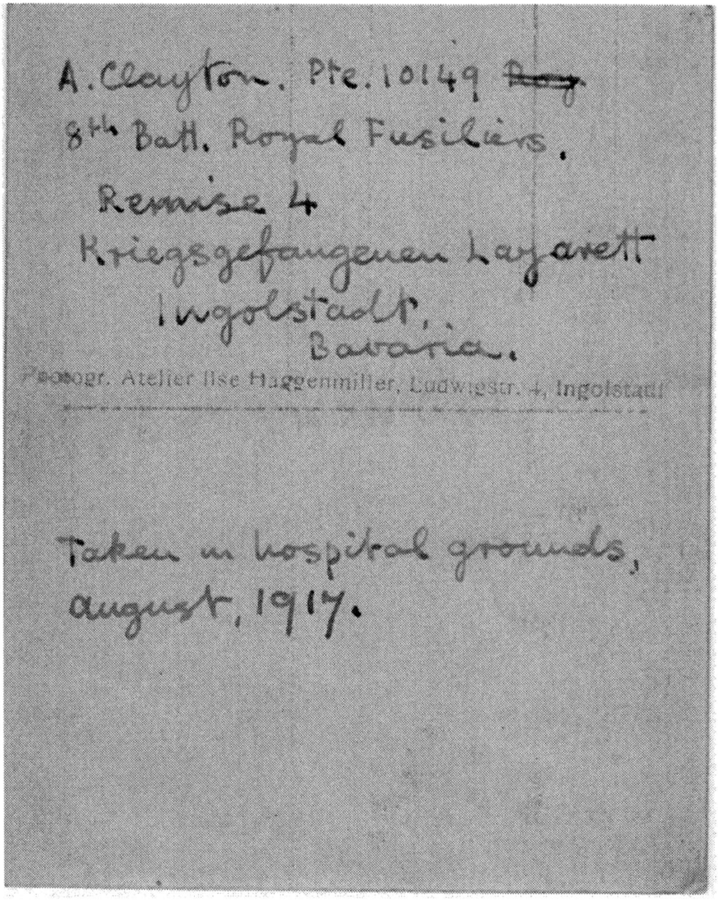
A. Clayton. Pte. 10149
8th Batt. Royal Fusiliers.
Remise 4
Kriegsgefangenen Lazarett
Ingolstadt,
Bavaria.
Photogr. Atelier Ilse Haggenmiller, Ludwigstr. 4, Ingolstadt

Taken in hospital grounds,
august, 1917.

Reverse of photograph in Albert's writing
'Kriegsgefangenen' – Prisoner of War; 'Lazarett' – military hospital

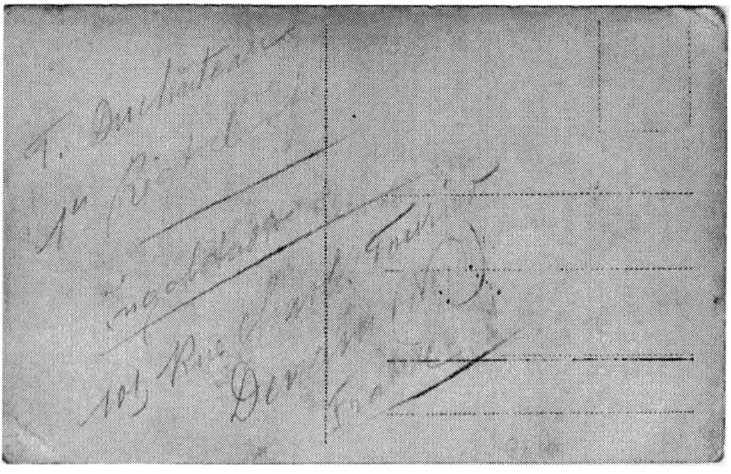

Reverse of photograph top right

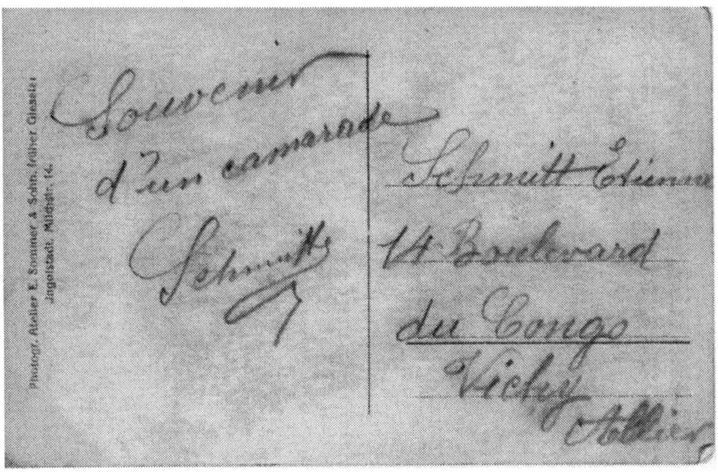

Reverse of group photo above

Albert Clayton - self portrait

www.longbeforedaybreak.com

For further information, comment and conversation.

Printed in Great Britain
by Amazon

60697095R00131